W9-CCH-898

Designing
Effective
Women's
Ministries

Designing Effective Women's Ministries

Choosing, Planning, and Implementing
the Right Programs for Your Church

JILL BRISCOE,
LAURIE KATZ MCINTYRE
& BETH SEVERSEN

ZondervanPublishingHouse
Grand Rapids, Michigan

A Division of HarperCollinsPublishers

Designing Effective Women's Ministries

Copyright © 1995 by Jill Briscoe, Laurie Katz McIntyre, and Beth Seversen. Queries may be addressed to Zondervan Publishing House, Grand Rapids, Michigan 49530.

Library of Congress Cataloging-in-Publication Data

Briscoe, Jill.
    Designing effective women's ministries : choosing, planning, and implementing the right programs for your church / Jill Briscoe, Laurie Katz McIntyre, and Beth Seversen.
      p. cm.
    Includes index.
    ISBN 0–310–43191–3 (pbk.)
    1. Church work with women. I. McIntyre, Laurie Katz, 1961– . II. Seversen, Beth Donigan. III. Title.
    BV4445.B75 1995   94–44260
    259'.082—dc20   CIP

Edited by Shauna Perez
Interior Design by Sherri L. Hoffman

Printed in the United States of America

00 01 /❖ DC/ 20 19 18 17 16 15 14 13 12 11 10 9 8

DEDICATED TO

the leaders of Elmbrook Women's Ministries,
past, present, and future, who,
blessed to be a blessing,
have so generously invested so much
of their heart, soul, and mind
in women's lives.

Contents

Prologue   9
Acknowledgments   11

Part I: BEGINNING A WOMEN'S MINISTRY

1. The Best Way to Begin Is to Begin   15
2. Start With What You've Got   23
3. Designing a Ministry Through Brainstorming   39
   Perspective: *Are You a Doer or a Dreamer?*   46
4. Put It All Together   49

Part II: MEETING WOMEN WHERE THEY LIVE

5. Morning Break   57
   Perspective: *Commitment to the Same Faces*   65
6. Moms and More   67
   Perspective: *Quiet Times in Noisy Times*   81
7. Evening Edition   83
   Perspective: *Women Wearing Many Hats*   90
8. The Widow's Might   93

Part III: DEVELOPING YOUR LEADERS

9. The Coordinator's Board   97
10. Looking for and Leading Your Leaders   101
11. Effective Leadership Retreats   123

Part IV: REACHING YOUR WORLD

12. Breakaway for Renewal   145
    Perspective: *Ask No Quarter*   164

13. Reaching Out through Special Events   167
    Perspective: *Between Your Own Two Feet*   188
14. Women on a Mission   191

Part V: Energizing Your Ministry

15. Being Women of Prayer   203

    Epilogue: Women Who Change Their World   215
    Appendix 1: Caring for a Speaker   217
    Appendix 2: Surveys and Forms   219

Prologue

❧

This book was written by several people who have invested their lives and hearts into ministry to women at Elmbrook Church in Waukesha, Wisconsin. For many years we have been nurturing the dream of sharing our experiences in women's ministries through a book such as this one, in the hope that many women will find themselves encouraged, challenged, and called by God to establish vibrant and life-giving ministries in their own churches. Over the last two decades we have seen God use our ministries to meet the needs of women, to train and equip them for leadership, and to lead many into new relationships with him. As witnesses of the great things that God has accomplished through and in women, how could we keep silent about all he has taught us?

This handbook is our combined effort to introduce to you the Elmbrook Church Women's Ministries as one model of ministry to women. We are not proposing that you adopt our exact model. Ours is simply a model of growth, not of perfection. Our hope, rather, is that our ideas and insights from the last twenty-five years of ministry will help you catch a vision for what God can do through a ministry to women. He transforms lives; he builds deeper relationships; he stretches us and teaches us, building into us the character of Christ. And we believe that the church as a whole can be built up as women are built up through women's ministries that are designed to meet their real needs.

Whether you are organizing or reorganizing your ministry to women, we invite you to window shop among the pages of ideas in this book. Our successes and failures will be shared in hopes that the former will inspire you and the latter may prevent you from repeating some of our mistakes! Program ideas, philosophies, structures, and principles which we have found helpful will be presented for your consideration. This book is intended to be a workbook. The wide margins make it convenient to take notes, brainstorm and put down ideas. If we can assist you in determining the needs and desires of the women in your church and community and serve as a catalyst for vital, vibrant ministries, tailor-made to address those needs and desires, then our purposes for writing this handbook will have been accomplished.

Women are creative, innovative, sensitive, gifted, nurturing, resourceful, and resilient! God knows that's true because he made us. We wish you all the joy and excitement we have found to be a part of ministering to women in his name.

Acknowledgments

It takes a certain type of woman to invest her life in the lives of her kind. It takes a woman with a heart for the Lord and for women's well-being to start with. It also takes a commitment to follow through, see to all the details, and deal with all the discouragements along the way.

The people who have contributed to this handbook are such women. This work reflects only a fraction of their expertise. God has developed a ministry that has touched hundreds of lives over the years, and we have learned in the growing to look first for his "well done" at the end of the day. It is fitting, however, to affirm and appreciate each other as well, and so we thank the loving friends and fellow "givers" and "doers" for having such a vital part of this big project. We trust it will be a catalyst in other women's lives.

The following women have contributed to the content of this handbook: Lisa Kinakin, Jennifer Johnson, Dell Jansen, Cindy Greenup, Carma Bowerman, Jean Robinson, Deb Hackbarth, and Janet Keddie.

Special editors have shaped it: Ann Lawton, Iva Johnson Danielson, and Shauna Perez.

Project support has been given by Elmbrook Women's Ministry board, and typists Laura Hintz, Ruth Dalbey, Rosie Nieznanski, and Debbie Briscoe have committed it efficiently to type.

Above all, we have all had a part in praying that the kingdom may come in many women's hearts because of their self-giving dedication and their delight in service—and their love for the Lord.

JILL BRISCOE

Part I

BEGINNING A WOMEN'S MINISTRY

Chapter 1

The Best Way to Begin Is to Begin

It was November 1970, and Stuart and I had just arrived in the U.S.A. I was thirty-five and scared, but it helped to have our three kids demanding special attention. We wanted them to adjust well, and that meant I worked hard to be positive about everything. Even the two-foot snowfall that arrived almost as soon as we did was the cause of laughter and family fun as we began to get our first taste of the Wisconsin winter.

We had never seen so much snow, and we had never seen so many people in church either. What a thrill! I well remember looking around at all the men in church. That was a shock to my system. I was used to being in Europe where the few people in church were, all too often, elderly women. How neat to see all these full grown men worshipping God, I thought. I was glad my children were observing this phenomena, so they would not get the idea that Christianity was only for old women and children!

The women in our congregation were wonderful! Not that I was interested in spending too much time with them, of course. I had my own plans. Having been involved with teenagers ever since I had become a Christian at the age of eighteen, I had brought lots of love to the "new country" to share from the "old country." It never occurred to me that God might have other

DESIGNING EFFECTIVE WOMEN'S MINISTRIES   15

things in mind for me. Apparently, though, it had occurred to some of the women I was about to meet.

A smart, attractive woman came calling almost as soon as I had unpacked. "Your husband told us—right from the pulpit—to drop by," she began cheerfully. "I wondered if you'd be interested in teaching a Bible study for a group of my friends and neighbors?" she continued.

Well, now, I thought, what can I say? It didn't sound as if the project would take too much of my time, and she seemed a very nice lady. While I was settling in and beginning to get to know the teenagers around the church and in the neighborhood, I reckoned I could take an hour or two a week to do that. As long as I chose something simple to teach that wouldn't take too much preparation and as long as the ladies all smiled as sweetly as this one was smiling at me, it didn't seem too frightening a prospect at all. So the dye was cast.

The very first week I realized I was in over my head. I felt as if everyone in the small group must have won some intelligence award from a prestigious college! Few knew much about the simple evangelical principles I had taken for granted. And they did not accept them as readily as I had done. Rather, they challenged my ideas. They had good reason for their arguments, they said. What was more, even though they all smiled at me, I found myself intimidated by their seeming self-confidence and the highly intellectual approach to truth and faith. Gone were the easy answers. These ladies had beautiful minds and gave me one big beautiful headache every week! I began to work harder than I had ever worked in my life, finding answers for each week's questions, preparing thoroughly instead of relying on someone else's material, praying up a storm for blessing, and feeling as though I was drowning. And all the time I didn't even want to do it!

I had some pretty petulant times with God complaining about it, too. Why did he let me get involved in the first place, I wondered? This was not my thing, and he must know it. I didn't understand women and their meetings, especially American women and their desire to identify with a group.

Yet one thing I knew from past experience. If God was in it, I had better shape up and get willing to do my part. I couldn't imagine he would want me to work with women for very long; but until he replaced me, I supposed he could hold the fort.

If God was in it, I had better shape up and get willing to do my part.

And so I dug in. I got out my little spade of faith and dug a trench on the front line of battle. We invited the bunch of friends we had gathered (the six had become sixty by now) to invite their friends or their enemies or both. Moving out of the lovely home in which we had started the group, we rented the basement of a local bank in a small shopping center.

The first thing I discovered about working with women was that I was one! Now that isn't a facetious remark, either. Believing I could never serve women because I didn't understand their needs was a trick the devil had played on me. That had only been an excuse. All I had to do was figure out "my" needs and how God could meet them and then learn how to press the need button for other women as well. I discovered that God and I were in business. Secondly, I learned that if I was to work with women, I would never run out of material. Half the human race were women! Women were everywhere.

It was a bit like having a baby. As soon as I knew I was pregnant, I was suddenly aware of baby buggies; I found myself peering into them and was surprised to experience a huge personal interest born in my heart. When God birthed his concern in me for women, it was as if I woke up to a whole new dimension of life and ministry.

Now it was merely a matter of being obedient. "As long as I can still work with the teenagers, Lord," I remember saying with complete confidence (he would never deny me that), "then I'm happy to turn my hand to this little matter of women's ministry for a little while."

But I was soon to learn it was *not* for a little while; and it was not a little matter, either. People—and women are certainly people—are no little matter to God. He cares for women as surely as he cares for men, and he wants them to know his intimate concern and his saving grace in their lives.

By now it was very obvious to many of us that God did indeed care for women. He was making that very evident by bringing more and more of them along every week. The bank building was full, and it was time to move again. We didn't have to look very far to know where to go. In the same shopping center there was a movie theater. "Could we use the theater in the morning for a Bible study?" we requested. "And how much would it

All I had to do was figure out "my" needs and how God could meet them and then learn how to press the need button for other women as well.

cost?" We were told we could have it when we liked, and it would cost little more than the price of a good family meal out!

It wasn't exactly easy, sitting in the semi-dark, sticking to the chewing gum and pop on the floor, and lugging the coffee clutter and boxes of books and materials there and back every week, but it was done. The day the huge urn full of coffee overturned in my friend's car reminded us of the advantage of permanent facilities! It was not that we didn't have a church building, but we had discerned the usefulness of neutral ground. To meet outside church allowed us to share our discoveries with many more women than if we had limited ourselves to our own church building and our own church women. By this time we had attracted all sorts of women from all sorts of church backgrounds with all sorts of needs and began to see the necessity for all sorts of programs to meet them.

One thing followed another. We simply started where we were with what we had and did the thing we discerned God wanted us to do. And what did we have to work with? One reluctant teacher (me) and a group of six eager women coming from all sorts of starting points, but all bound and determined to journey towards God. That's all the Lord needs. He works with us all where we are, not where he wishes we were. He doesn't wait until the teacher is mature enough or until the listeners have got their doctrine straight and are willing to do their homework. He takes us all just where we are and says, "Let's begin." And the best way to begin is to begin. Not necessarily to pray long about it, or to form a committee and talk about it for months, or even to raise funds to pay for it first, but just begin! The prayer will be more meaningful, the committee will rise up from among the helpers, and the money will come if God is in it. You'll see. Take the first step. And let that first step be a step and not a huge leap into space!

You see, God doesn't want us to wait until we are fit to go to the Olympics before we take our first faltering step of faith. He wants us to take a little step of obedience, that's all!. Just a quick, unsteady, tottering step toward the will of God as you see it. Don't worry if you don't want to take the step, if you feel unworthy, or ignorant, or too young, or too old, or too middle-aged, or too encumbered with kids, or too anything! Look up and discern God's will. What is he telling you to do for someone

We simply started where we were with what we had and did the thing we discerned God wanted us to do.

else? What is the need you see right under your nose? When you've figured that out, don't worry about finishing the job, just worry about the first step. Concentrate on that. The other steps will take care of themselves.

I have observed that, so often, the walk of faith never takes the walker anywhere because the walker won't start unless she thinks she can win. I believe with all my heart that all God asks of us is to take the *next* step. Now for some of us the next step is the first step. For others it's the 101st step or the 1000th. But the next step is the most important one for all of us, because without it we can never take the next, and the next, and the next, up to the last and final step of the will of God into his arms!

For me, the first step toward this particular need was to respond to a woman's request to meet with a small group of women and teach them. For that particular woman, her first step towards God's will for her life was to ask me to teach them! The exciting thing about taking the next step along God's time line for our lives is bumping into so many people along the way who are busy taking their next steps. It's great fun! You can even help each other figure out what's next, or take the step with them to encourage them, or suggest someone else to be their companion.

After three years of next steps, there were four hundred of us. We all put our arms around each other's faltering faith, rented a movie theater, and planted our feet firmly and squarely in God's plan for women in our hometown. What joy! By the time we had been there another year or two, three hundred more ladies had joined us and we were seven hundred strong.

The thing about all of this is you never know who will be walking by your side. Sometimes it's lonely and sometimes it's pretty crowded along that straight street. For the first few months of my adventure in faith with women, I felt very alone. There were so many, but I was shy and still adjusting to a new culture and country. I couldn't get over the sneaking feeling they didn't like the way I dressed (a concept encouraged by continual helpful hints about my appearance!) or the way I lived my life. I was different because I didn't seem to enjoy the things all women should enjoy, like shopping (actually I loved shopping, but had had little money for so long that I had completely lost my appetite for it) or having lunch together (how many calories can you add in a week?). I really began to believe they only liked me

All God asks of us is to take the *next* step.

You never know who will be walking by your side. Sometimes it's lonely and sometimes it's pretty crowded along that straight street.

for my teaching. And in the end, that is all that matters. They liked Jesus, and I could help them take the next step toward him. It was this particular joy that released me from expending time and energy in gaining personal popularity. For me, it was a big step!

I was expecting to stop soon. After all, I had believed this was a temporary expedient until the Lord brought along the right woman for the job. But the Holy Spirit had been whispering in my ear that I was the right woman for the job, and other voices joined in the chorus of conviction. I had seen the need of women around me, started to try and meet that need, met it in some measure, only to encounter ten more needs that no one was meeting!

So now I asked myself again four years later, thinking back to 1970, "Why have a women's ministry?" The format of our program hadn't changed much at all since we had begun. It consisted of a Bible lecture sandwiched between a little singing and coffee. The women began to let me know they were hungry for more than a sandwich! But why should they expect me to provide an entire meal?

It was 1974, and women had begun to trek back to the work place. It was hardly perceptible at first. I began to notice only after my committee had noticeably thinned out. Now these women began to make me aware of new needs they discovered as they began to juggle home, family, and career as best they could. On the other hand, young mothers among us who were still at home were exhausted from carting their children off to baby-sitting facilities far away from the theater. They also needed the support of practical biblical principles for the home and family. Then the committee needed to develop their own skills in order to build up the women around them. It was time for a re-evaluation from all of us.

It was tempting to stay put. After all, "If it ain't broke, don't fix it." But if cracks start appearing in the structure, it's foolish to hang around until the whole thing disintegrates. It did rather put me on the spot, however. God speaks in many ways, not least with the big strong voice of duty, reminding us that if we have taken on a God-given responsibility, we had better have a God-given reason to drop it at any stage of the game! I could find no God-given reason. In fact, my reluctance to involve myself in a service area I did not consider myself gifted or interested in had long since been replaced by a "ready, steady, go" attitude. I was "ready," working on being "steady," and waiting for the starting gun for the next stage of the race. I had never dreamed I would have a heart for women. I didn't doubt that I had a heart for kids. But for their mothers?! Of course, if I'd waited till I felt the heartbeat, I would never have begun at all. Love comes as we serve, as we get involved, as we work closely together. We need to be near enough to see the tears, to catch the sign, to touch each other's hand. Now I didn't want out anymore. I was ready for the next step. And what a challenge that turned out to be!

JILL BRISCOE

Love comes as we serve.

Chapter 2

Start With What You've Got

This handbook was written by people involved in women's ministries at Elmbrook Church. Our goal is to share what we have learned in the hope that it will inspire others to develop their own models for ministry to women. Although we will refer frequently to the ministries at Elmbrook, we want to assure you that these references simply serve to illustrate the principles we have discovered about ministering to women. We hope you will enjoy browsing through our closet of programs, philosophies and ideas, trying on and keeping the ones that fit your women best.

ASKING THE BIG QUESTION

More than fifteen years had passed since Jill, quite by accident, first began the women's ministries at Elmbrook. She handed the responsibilities over to Beth Seversen, our first Women's Ministries Pastor, in 1987. The ministry had diversified and many exciting programs for women were flourishing. It gradually dawned upon the leadership that we had never determined *why* we were doing what we were doing. All kinds of ministries were springing up. How much should we take on? Was it possible to diversify too much? Could we support all these ministries and still do all of them well? Would maintaining all this growth hurt our unity? These are but a sample of the issues we faced.

We realized that we needed to pinpoint and clarify our primary purpose as a starting point. Without a clear understanding of our ultimate task, priorities were fuzzy, and decision-making was difficult. Writing a purpose statement helped us delineate our goal clearly. A purpose statement concisely articulates what a ministry intends to accomplish in one or two sentences. Such a statement can work powerfully to illuminate the focus of a ministry, both for the leaders and participants.

When a purpose statement is prominent in your literature, a woman reading your brochure will know exactly what the organization is, its purpose, and its direction.

Here is the purpose statement we created for Elmbrook:

The Elmbrook Church Women's Ministries emphasize women ministering to women for the purpose of encouraging, equipping and evangelizing women in Milwaukee, the Midwest, the United States, and across the globe.

A purpose statement should reflect a balanced program of fellowship, nurture, equipping, and evangelism. Inreach (by which we mean helping women mature in their faith) and outreach are both essential to a healthy women's ministry. The purpose statement provides a measure for your ministry. If you know what you want to accomplish, then programs and ideas can be evaluated and determined by your purpose statement. Purpose statements need to be periodically re-evaluated and revised as the needs of your ministry change. They should accurately reflect your ministry. Otherwise, either the ministry or the statement should be changed.

Hammering out a purpose statement is not difficult. You might want to invite either a leadership team or all the women interested in women's ministries in your church to a purpose statement brainstorming session. Ask each woman to bring along a one-sentence statement of what she believes is or should be the purpose of the women's ministries. At the session divide the women into groups of three or four and allow time for small group prayer for God's leadership and unity. Then ask the women to share their prepared sentences with their small groups. Allow twenty minutes for each group to consolidate their ideas and agree upon a one-sentence purpose statement. Bringing all the small groups back together again, have each small group share theirs aloud, and write these on the board or overhead for all to see. Then as a large group, formulate a one- or two-sentence statement which precisely describes the intent of your ministry. Since the large group is working toward establishing the "big picture" for the ministry, it's a good idea for the group to appoint someone who can "fine tune" the statement, to check grammar and to prayerfully consider how it might be worded more smoothly or succinctly. Prayer should be a key element in each step of the process.

A question women's ministry leaders often ask is, "How do you keep your women united?" One answer is to involve women in the decision-making process, giving them ownership and responsibility. You can be assured that if the members help you work out a purpose statement and help design the ministry, they are more likely to back it with full support and attendance.

CHECKPOINT

1. Have you defined the purpose of your women's ministry and designed a purpose statement?
2. Has your purpose been effectively communicated to the women in your ministry?
3. Were the women involved in the designing of your purpose statement?
4. Do your current women's ministries adequately reflect your purpose statement?
5. If you have a purpose statement, has it recently been evaluated?
6. Does your purpose statement adequately reflect the needs of your women and community?

ASSESSING YOUR NEEDS

We have discovered some practical tools for keeping our leadership in touch with the ever-changing needs of women. Successes and failures over the years have taught us that evaluation is essential for an effective ministry and a healthy program.

Evaluation is the basis for continuing change, the foundation for a growing ministry. Unfortunately, change is often met with resistance. How then can a ministry accurately assess its needs and institute necessary change?

Imagine for a moment that your last women's event ends the year, and the start of the new fiscal year is just around the corner. In a matter of a few short months your Women's Ministries will again be gearing up for the fall. At the quarterly planning meeting you excitedly gather with your committee to begin brainstorming and praying for the upcoming year.

"We could have a series on family relationships and the Bible," offers one woman.

"Or how about an overnight getaway where women can be both physically and spiritually refreshed?" says another.

"No, I think what we really need is a weekly Bible study for working women dealing with relevant biblical issues," adds another.

The women explode with enthusiasm and further discussion.

"Now all we need is to begin forming our committees so we can get started," says another.

Does this scene seem strangely familiar? Frequently, this type of session results in a number of great and workable ideas, but with little promise of producing a ministry that will make a spiritual difference in the women you hope to reach. Why? Because the planning is program-focused instead of people-focused.

To be effective, you have to know who it is you're working with and ministering to. A working women's Bible study may be a great idea, but what if the majority of your women are stay-at-home moms with small children? People must be the primary consideration, and programming should always come *second*. After all, ministry *is* people.

How can you better understand women's changing needs and roles today? How can you keep current and relevant—meeting women where they truly live? If you want to establish a women's ministry that is vitally connected to the actual needs of women in your church and community, a "people study" can be a terrific starting point.

Research experts tell us we must regularly be asking and answering questions such as:

Who are we trying to reach?

> **Evaluation is the basis for continuing change, the foundation for a growing ministry.**

> **People must be the primary consideration, and programming should always comes *second*.**

Who is actually being reached?

Who is absent? Why?

How has our audience changed?

What are their greatest needs?

What are our current barriers to ministry and how can they be removed?

What are our greatest strengths and weaknesses?

In what areas do we need to change?

A careful look at several research methods (such as expert opinion, written surveys, phone surveys, and focus group discussions) and their specific uses will be helpful in establishing a ministry, as well as aiding on-going ministry analysis.

Meeting Assumed Needs

The first assessment tool is known as "expert opinion." In this case, an individual (i.e., pastor or director) or group of individuals (i.e., board or committee) makes decisions on behalf of a group with little or no input from the target audience. Examples of decisions made based on expert opinion include grade school curriculum development, college accreditation, and preaching. For instance, a women's Bible-study committee or head teacher normally decides the next teaching series based on what they, the experts, think the group needs. Rarely do they take it to the ministry for a vote!

A word of explanation regarding perceived and assumed needs may be helpful here. A perceived need is one that people feel and recognize, such as the need for laughter, friendship, and prayer. An assumed need may not necessarily be felt or recognized. For instance, the Scriptures tell us that believers are to discover and use their gifts in service to Christ. Not all believers are using their gifts, and many do not feel driven to do so; however, as a Christian leader you know that learning to use one's gifts is not only a command but a need, an assumed need. In order to meet this assumed need, you may choose to include opportunities for serving in your program. You realize the importance of this need, whether others do or not. Obviously, determining assumed needs is more difficult than discovering perceived needs, but a ministry that strives to meet both will be a deeper ministry.

Advantages
- Creates no unfulfilled expectations
- Allows for long term planning
- Allows the ministry "experts" to determine the ministry's direction
- Addresses perceived and assumed needs

Disadvantages
- Lack of ownership or "buy in"
- Dependent on perceptions and judgments of leaders/experts

Special Instructions
- Determine target audience needs
- Keep an eye on society (magazines, TV)
- Talk to other experts/leaders
- Recognize that people vote with their feet—if you offer what people want, they *will* come

The expert opinion method is best used for planning an overall program, setting long-range goals, and establishing the basic direction for your ministry. It is not intended to be an exclusive evaluation tool.

Gathering Breadth of Information

The second and most commonly used assessment tool is a written survey. Written surveys should be designed to gather *breadth* of information rather than *depth* of information. They are an excellent tool for gathering *concrete* information and are a useful first step for launching a deeper study based on what the data collected reveal.

Advantages
- Comparatively easy to develop and review
- Can be administered to large groups

Disadvantage
- Generally only useful in obtaining demographic or very limited, concrete types of information

Have you ever been handed a survey and groaned when you realized that you were being asked to think, evaluate, and then formulate words to communicate exactly what you want to con-

Written surveys should be designed to gather *breadth* of information rather than *depth* of information.

vey to the surveyors? It is difficult to communicate opinions beyond yes or no on paper. Yet the biggest mistake made when
using surveys as an assessment tool is just that—using them to
obtain opinions, evaluation, or information dependent on issues.
It is unrealistic to expect an audience to squeeze out complex,
high-brain function thinking in five to ten minutes! A survey
should be designed to include direct, easy-to-answer questions
that can be completed with few words in a relatively short time.
The length of the survey itself is not necessarily an issue; it is the
amount of time it takes to complete it.

Other common mistakes made when writing surveys include:

- Defining your audience too broadly or narrowly
- Including too much in the survey
- Writing questions that are vague and ambiguous
- Reviewing data insufficiently
- Administering survey poorly—e.g., giving a survey to tired people at the end of a retreat
- Surveying too often or too seldom (once every two years is adequate)

One of the most effective surveys that we've used is our
yearly Partnership Survey. Although it is several pages long, it can
be completed in a short time span as women are invited to simply check off areas of ministry in which they would like to help.
This survey serves a two-fold purpose. It invites women to use
their talents, skills and abilities for ministry, and it provides a resource list of women who we can call for committee positions,
event planning or volunteer work. Our partnership survey has
been invaluable for increasing involvement and recruitment (see
appendix 2).

Special Instructions

- Create and sustain audience participation through attrac-
tive survey design and careful survey administration
- Be wary of paper overload, distractions and limited atten-
tion spans
- Keep it simple, easy, and brief
- Consider giving a gift for completed surveys
- Remember, surveys are designed to gather concrete infor-
mation, not to evaluate ministry

> **The length of the survey itself is not necessarily an issue; it is the amount of time it takes to complete it.**

Gathering Depth of Information

Phone surveys provide a more personal opportunity for interaction, allowing respondents the time and setting to clarify their evaluations. They can accomplish what written surveys cannot—directed discussion and analysis through interaction. An opportune time to use this method would be as a follow-up to a women's conference or retreat. Instead of asking tired women to express their opinions on paper, randomly call 20% of the attendees and solicit their observations over the phone once they are rested and recovered. Phone surveys can also be used to research causes for dwindling participation in a ministry. People who have dropped out of a ministry will never be reached by an "in-house" written survey. Phone calls can show them that the women in the church care about them, miss them, and value their opinions and input.

Advantages
- Can reach a moderately large audience
- Allows for open-ended questions, follow-up questions, and probing by the caller
- Can address issues as well as concrete information

Disadvantages
- Labor intensive
- Complicated
- Dependent on skills of callers

Special instructions
- Clearly define the information you need before you begin
- Respect participants' time
- Run a pilot study with your questions
- Train callers
- Do not tape calls unless you have legal permission

Small-Group Verbal Surveys

By now you might be wondering which assessment tool is most helpful for gathering opinions, collecting new ideas and creating strategic plans. In our experience, the best way to accomplish these goals is through something we call focus-group discussions.

The main objective of focus-group discussion is problem solving. Five to twelve people participate in a discussion led by a facilitator, covering a variety of pre-determined topics. In essence, a focus-group discussion is a written survey done verbally in a small group, directed by a pre-appointed leader who records the group's responses and suggestions. A focus-group discussion is similar to a market research study group.

For a focus group to be effective, single out an issue or several realistic problems to be solved. For instance, our working women's ministry conducted a focus group discussion in order to develop a new evening Bible study format. Our young mothers' group pulled women together to discuss scheduling, creative program planning, and nursery difficulties. Sample focus-group questions are shown on page 32.

The focus group participates in a one- to two-hour brainstorming and problem-solving session. Some women can be randomly asked while others may want to volunteer. Encourage participation by emphasizing that each woman's opinions and ideas are invaluable and assure them that it will be an enjoyable, interactive time. We've learned not to overload any particular group with committee members, as it can be threatening to other participants and prevent honest sharing. It is not necessary to include all the women in your group or church. Statistics indicate that if 20 percent of a group's population participates in a written survey or group discussion, it accurately reflects the whole.

The facilitator in a focus-group discussion plays a strategic role. She will need to create an inviting atmosphere, encourage participation, and direct the conversation to fruitful ends, keeping the discussion from disintegrating into a pool of negativism or criticism. Although evaluation naturally includes pointing out areas that need improvement, constructive criticism leads to problem-solving, rather than complaining.

The facilitator's role is to

- Meet, greet, and make participants comfortable (consider coffee and refreshments)
- Pray
- Restate the purpose of the group
- Set the stage: Opinions are important, but not every idea can/will be implemented

> **The main objective of focus-group discussion is problem solving.**

QUESTIONS FOR FOCUS GROUP
DISCUSSION—AN EXAMPLE

Facilitator records all responses and asks group if individual experiences represent general experiences. Facilitator also draws out responses, particularly for topics not specifically being addressed.

1. What is your most vivid memory of Moms and More (M & M) this year? This memory can be positive or negative and can have anything at all to do with your M & M experience.
2. I've listed our speakers and their topics on this chart. What memories do you have of these speaker weeks?
3. This year we focused on biblical exposition during our speaker weeks rather than on specific topics (explain "biblical exposition," giving example of topical subject). What did you think of this approach?
4. Would you like to see the same approach used next year? Would you prefer topics?
5. What topics would you like to hear covered? And what speakers would you like to address them?
   [If the group can't think of topics, the facilitator offers examples, one at a time.]
6. What have been the strengths and weaknesses of your small-group experience this year?
   Special Events
   Platform
   Bible Study Groups
   Child Care
7. What would make M & M better? (Brainstorm)
8. Would you bring an unsaved friend, neighbor or relative to M & M? If yes, to what kind of event? If no, why not?
9. Have you known anyone who began attending M & M this year but didn't complete the year? Why did she stop attending?
   [Facilitator gets a list of names and reasons, including "unknown."]

- Follow a list of predetermined questions, but be willing to deviate if useful and necessary
- Start with general ideas and progress to specifics
- Keep brainstorming on track
- Avoid criticism of the leaders or the group as a whole
- Determine if an individual's thoughts, feelings, or experiences are shared by the group
- Base evaluation questions on experience rather than theory
- Record responses of participants on flip chart or blackboard so everyone can see

Advantages
- Maximum participant "buy in"
- Dynamic, interactive process promotes problem-solving and sharing of ideas
- Small, intimate groups encourage participation, bring out positive and negative analysis
- Less threatening than writing to most people

Disadvantages
- Time-consuming
- Dependent on skilled facilitator

Special Instructions
- Make it fun to participate
- Make it an honor to participate
- Establish realistic expectations for the group's opinions and recommendations
- Create a sense of openness and creativity

We have integrated focus-group discussions into every aspect of our ministry and have applied many of the principles to our committee meetings. Focus-group discussions are especially useful for fledgling ministries or churches who are trying to establish a new ministry. Questions such as "What would you like to see included in our ministry?" and "What, in your opinion, are the three greatest needs facing women today?" are excellent starting points for such groups.

Focus groups can also revitalize a ministry that has lost its effectiveness or bridge gaps between opposing groups. For instance, one women's group saw a widening gap between its older and younger women and brought together representatives from each group to confront and solve the problems, rather than allow walls to grow thicker. Because the focus-group technique worked so well, unity was restored and teamwork began!

Ongoing ministry effectiveness requires constant evaluation. Many tools are available, but these need to be appropriately applied in order to accurately assess needs and affect change. Don't let evaluation overwhelm you. Change, though not pain-free, can add tremendous spark and impetus to a faltering ministry or fine-tune a successful ministry.

In the same way evaluation benefits ministry, carefully planning programs and events can produce fantastic results. When events are based on data gained through research and problem-solving, programming can go far in stimulating Christ-like growth among the women in your group.

The following practical "how-to's" are organized in outline form to help you, your ministry team, and church women design an ongoing ministry or a special event from start to finish. (Think of yourself as the facilitator in this process, not the leader.) This outline can also be used directly with your brainstorming groups as they work to contribute ideas for the development of a new or special ministry.

DESIGNING A MINISTRY

Four ingredients are necessary when considering a new ministry venture or a special event. Whether you are considering an ongoing Bible study or a single retreat, these four guidelines are essential to a well-thought-out program.

A. Decide on Your Purpose
1. *Write a one-sentence purpose statement* (see p. 24 for a sample). Discuss your objectives, vision, and needs.
2. *Select your methods and your strategy.* In the past, our ministry to working women held evangelistic lunches. A workmate was invited to a lovely luncheon where a speaker's address wove the gospel throughout the message. Lunch-hour Bible studies were advertised at these evangelistic lunches for follow up. These were thirty-minute studies located in the marketplace—anyplace where women work: an office building, a bank, a mall, a hospital, and so on. If a friend indicated an interest at the luncheon, she was then in-

> Change, though not pain-free, can add tremendous spark and impetus to a faltering ministry or fine-tune a successful ministry.

vited to attend a six-week beginner's Bible study. In this example, the method for reaching unchurched and non-Christian working women for Christ was to host evangelistic luncheons. The strategy was to funnel these women into Bible studies in their own locations that would cover topics such as "How to Become a Christian" and "How to Live the Christian Life."

3. *Establish your philosophies.* Example a: Our women's ministries seek to promote an attitude that encourages women to attempt new ventures and allows them the freedom to fail. Example b: We believe that women should be selected for leadership through "shoulder tapping," and only on rare occasions by election.

4. *Adopt your policies.* Many of these are hammered out over the years, but some will need to be established from the beginning. One policy we maintain is that our outside speakers are asked to review our statement of faith and sign a paper saying they will not veer from or take issue with our church dogma. Our financial and honorarium policies follow.

> **We seek to promote an attitude that encourages women to attempt new ventures and allows them the freedom to fail.**

FINANCIAL POLICY

1. We are self-supporting, and only the pastor's salary, intern, and resident salaries are included in the general budget.
2. The Council of Elders has allowed us the freedom to take offerings, ask for donations, and to charge for events.
3. All fundraising ideas must be submitted to the Associate Pastor of Women's Ministries, and she in turn asks the pastoral staff for approval.
4. We are careful never to do anything that we cannot afford.
5. Each year a dollar amount is given by the Coordinator's Board to three arms of the ministry: Morning Break, Evening Edition, and Moms and More, for the purpose of evangelism.

HONORARIUM POLICY

1. No in-house women are paid for anything in-house (e.g., speaking, music, crafts, aerobics).
2. We do not pay fees to our guest speakers, but offer honorariums in accordance with our conference budgets.
3. Each guest speaker is individually assessed. Considerations include: single, single parent, double income, student, receives her living by the gospel, etc. Traveling expenses are always reimbursed.

B. Develop your Program
   1. Assess your resources through prayer and brainstorming (e.g., teachers, musicians, speakers, facilities, friends)
   2. Select a theme (e.g., "Flying Solo" for a single-parenting event)
   3. Choose a format (e.g., weekly, biweekly, or monthly meeting; a luncheon, overnight, morning, or one-day event; seminars; and platform)
   4. Title the program
   5. Suggest locations
   6. Determine a date
   7. Prepare a budget
   8. Consider childcare

C. Delegate Responsibilities
   1. Establish committee positions (see page 50 for ideas)
   2. Recruit a team. Start with friends. Look for visionaries, encouragers, and detail people
   3. Set up a committee organizational chart that delineates communication, responsibility, and authority

D. Determine Your Calendar
   1. Outline what must be done by when, much like a bride's checklist
   2. Schedule future committee meetings and the date(s) of the ministry or event
   3. Make up a prayer calendar (see p. 210)
   4. Plan an evaluation/celebration meeting for soon after the ministry event

---

CHECKPOINT

1. Have you identified your target audience?
2. What method of assessing their perceived needs would best suit your situation?
3. How will you facilitate this method?
4. What does the leadership believe the assumed needs of your target audience are?
5. What are your methods, strategies, philosophies, and policies for beginning and maintaining Women's Ministries? Do all committee members know and understand them?
6. Have you determined your budget, and how it will be met?

Chapter 3

Designing a Ministry Through Brainstorming

One of the most difficult aspects of women's ministries is program planning. How do we get started? What kind of event should we feature? Who should we target? And who will help? These are just a few of the questions that arise when launching an effective women's program. The "Designing a Ministry" principles outlined in chapter 2 can be used as a great brainstorming tool with small groups. We've used these principles to get the ideas flowing by asking our brainstorming groups to pretend that they must plan an entire event or program in only thirty minutes! This is not the only way to generate ideas, but hopefully it will provide a springboard from which you can launch your own unique approach.

UNDERSTANDING BRAINSTORMING

Before you set your "brainstormers" in motion, make sure that you and your women have a firm understanding of the brainstorming concept. Brainstorming is a simple technique for quickly generating a long list of creative ideas. The goal in brainstorming is to generate numerous ideas or solutions to a problem by suspending criticism and evaluation until a later processing session. Share with your groups the following suggestions before turning them loose:

1. Accept and record *all* ideas
2. Do not comment on anyone else's ideas
3. Make no judgments
4. Accept repeated ideas and do not draw attention to the fact that an idea has already been suggested

Be Inclusive

When planning programs and events, involve as many participants as possible. Because brainstorming spreads enthusiasm, initial planning should not be limited to an exclusive few.

Invite anyone and everyone to come and share their ideas and pray together about the future ministry or event. Bulletin announcements are usually not enough. Women are more likely to participate as you do some persuasive "shoulder tapping." Spending time together first in fellowship at a coffee, light lunch, or potluck supper is a great way to encourage participation, and an effective way to help women relax and enjoy their time together.

After this time of fellowship, outline what you hope to accomplish and divide the women into groups of four to six, asking them to begin their small group time with about fifteen minutes of prayer for God's guidance in their task. You might want to share some devotional thoughts first.

Next, pass out these four questions and ask the women to ponder them silently for five minutes or so, and record their answers.

1. As a Christian woman, what is your greatest personal need or area in which you would like to see yourself grow at the present time?
2. Identify the two most prevalent needs of your closest non-Christian friend.
3. Thinking about the women in our church, what concerns do you have for them, and which group of women in our church do you believe need immediate attention (e.g., singles, single moms, widows, working women, moms, empty nesters, missionaries)?

> **Because brainstorming spreads enthusiasm, initial planning should not be limited to an exclusive few.**

4. Identify a pressing need or issue your community is facing. How could a ministry of our church help address this problem?

Now ask the women to share their answers in the groups and to prioritize the needs they have identified, selecting one they wish to tackle. Explain that each group has the task of planning a new ministry or special event for the purpose of meeting the need the group has collectively selected. They are to accomplish this by using the four guidelines outlined under the "Designing a Ministry" section in chapter 2:

1. Decide on your purpose
2. Develop your program
3. Delegate responsibilities
4. Determine your calendar

The results can be a one-time happening or an ongoing program. The women are to pretend that they are the members of the committee that will pull it all together. Do not panic if they look at you and say, "You've got to be kidding!"

You will want to walk them through the outline and monitor their time by interrupting every six or seven minutes and moving the groups on to the next point of the outline. Remind them that since they make up the committee, each one must volunteer for a position or two. Ask them to begin by selecting a chairperson (perhaps the person who has the most red on) and a secretary (whoever has a birthday closest to April 1). The secretary records *all* ideas and takes the committee's minutes. Allow thirty minutes for this exercise.

After the allotted time of brainstorming, ask each secretary to stand up and share aloud the ministry her group has brainstormed. Have her mention the need tackled, the method selected, the theme, program, and format, along with the date, and the committee positions each member assumed. Have a recorder volunteer to list each theme on a chalkboard or easel for all to see.

Women may surprise you with their inventiveness during this exercise. Jill and Beth used this method at a conference for pastor's wives in South Africa. One group created an event for single parents in their church called "Flying Solo." It was to be held on the church premises from 9:00 AM to 3:00 PM on a Saturday. Programming was provided for the attendees' children, rather than just baby-sitting services. A few months later this idea became a reality, and a keynote speaker and seminars addressed the needs of many single parents. The day was a significant milestone in the lives of single parents. In this case, a simple brainstorming session turned into a tremendous opportunity for ministry!

When the small groups are finished, you may be surprised to find a common thread running through their ideas. Prioritize them in categories such as the greatest need or the most feasible to attempt. Ask each group if they found an idea or two that they believed the Lord would have them accomplish in the coming year. Encourage group members to consider the importance of doing a few things well.

Collect all the recorders' notes and set a date when a chairperson and committee will go over and finalize the results of the brainstorming session. Some women will be so excited about the implementation of these new ideas that they will want to help carry them out. To help get them involved, pass around a sign-up sheet on which women can indicate their interest, noting their name, address, and phone number, along with the area in which they would like to serve.

Many women will experience a new sense of fulfillment in Christ when they participate in these brainstorming sessions as they realize how much they can do in God's strength. Brainstorming should introduce them to fresh program ideas while promoting enthusiasm for trying something new and different. Most importantly, they should encourage a sense of ownership by lay women for these new ventures and help them to see themselves as an integral part of the ministry team.

Exposing the Creativity Myth

Women often believe they are not creative. Most likely that thought was spawned by Satan, the father of lies. Perhaps what these women don't understand about creativity is that ideas come with practice. Thomas Edison said, "To have a good idea, have lots of them."

In "Ten Proven Methods for Hatching Brilliant Ideas," from the October 1985 *Republic* magazine, Robert Tucker states:

> The notion that ideas pop out of anyone's head fully developed and ready to be implemented makes for interesting mythology but it isn't supported by research.

In reality, most of the ideas an innovator comes up with are never acted on, they're REJECTED or evolve into better, stronger ideas.

The fact is, you are probably generating more ideas than you give yourself credit for. Everybody has ideas. Everybody has a certain amount of good ones. But not everybody WORKS with those ideas in such a way as to create new opportunities and solve problems. That's what sets innovators apart. They aren't the least bit interested in just having ideas for the sake of having them. They look at ideas as future realities.

Several principles from this article can help women to sprout new ideas and encourage them to use their creativity for God.

To come up with a good idea we must take the risk of having many of our ideas rejected. Get into the habit of telling yourself, "I've got lots of ideas, but only a few really good ones." Ask God to help you identify the really good ones. Challenge your leaders to risk a myriad of mediocre ideas in order to pursue those rare ideas that make all the brainstorming worthwhile. For if they never generate hundreds of mediocre ideas in the first place, their occasional strokes of brilliance will never be born.

Most ideas evolve!

This happens by adopting and adapting. Remember that Ecclesiastes says, "There is nothing new under the sun." Rarely do any of us come up with a completely original idea. Usually, we will build on someone else's idea and make it our own, or re-work it to fit our situation.

A few years ago Elmbrook Women's Ministries became troubled over the fact that one of our programs for women was dwindling in numbers. About that same time one of our missionaries returned home after serving for forty-two years in Africa. Our leadership was excited to learn that she had designed and written curriculum for a ministry called "Women of the Good News." Over the years this ministry had exploded and multiplied from the original five women to more than six thousand. We adopted several ideas from this African ministry, changed elements to fit our own group, and the result was a unique program that strengthened many of our weaknesses. These are the steps we took.

1. We recognized a problem and the need for a solution.
2. We invited Jean to share her program with us.

> **To come up with a good idea we must take the risk of having many of our ideas rejected.**

3. A sub-committee met to pray and discuss this new information over a period of months.

Jean's program slowly evolved into our own. The two programs shared both similarities and differences. This was just the boost our ministry needed.

Everybody has some good ideas.

This principle is convincing, particularly because each of us is created in the image of God, the Supreme Creator, and it is his Spirit who resides in us. The Spirit was God's creative agent in Genesis chapter 1. He lends us God's creativity. When a problem in ministry comes up, ask God for his creativity and ideas to solve it.

We must work with our ideas.

It takes prayer, hard work, and practice to come up with ideas. Musicians learn to play the piano with practice. Pastors learn to preach with practice. Sprouting new ideas takes practice, too. Every time someone asks you for a suggestion, try to think up ten instead of one. If a friend asks your suggestion for a gift for her father-in-law's birthday, for example, try giving her ten ideas. If you make this a habit, your idea-ability will greatly improve. Soon it will drive you crazy because you won't be able to turn your brain *off*.

Put feet on your ideas.

God gave us our imaginations to further his kingdom and to bring him glory. If we have an idea for ministry, we have a God-given responsibility to see that it gets off the ground. If we absolutely cannot do it ourselves, we should at least drop the baited hook in the pond and see if someone else would like to nibble on it. God calls us not only to "dream dreams," but also to do good works. We must do all we can to see that our God-given ideas become realities which enhance the Gospel of Christ.

Caution: Avoid negative people when sprouting new ideas!

Tucker says that "In their initial stages, ideas are seeds. They need nurture and encouragement to grow and mature. They definitely need to be examined and evaluated, but gently, not harshly." In our women's ministries we must try hard to be open to new ideas and examine our own hearts to ensure that they are

If we have an idea for ministry, we have a God-given responsibility to see that it gets off the ground.

not overly critical. Sometimes the first reaction to something new is, "Oh, that will never work because. . ." or "We tried that before and it didn't work." Instead of premature negativism, work hard to try and see the adventure in exploring new ideas optimistically. It is rewarding to help women get their ideas off the ground!

BUILDING ON YOUR GREATEST RESOURCE

The key to "Start with What You've Got" is simply this: build your ministry on the foundation God has already provided for you, the women in your church. Ministry must be designed according to your own women's specific characteristics and needs. Only as you uncover these qualities will you be able to design a women's ministry that is relevant and appropriate for your particular church and community. Intentionally designing your programs around women's needs will give your ministry the right foundation. Involving your women in the data-gathering, goal-setting, program-building, and brainstorming processes will insure that your ministry has the support and leadership it needs.

In our next chapter you will see how a small church, using the principles outlined in this chapter, started a women's ministry from scratch.

Instead of premature negativism, work hard to try and see the adventure in exploring new ideas optimistically.

CHECKPOINT

1. Is your approach to brainstorming exclusive or inclusive?
2. Are you and your committee members personally inviting at least two to three new women to your brainstorming meetings?
3. Are new ideas easily accepted by your committee?
4. What steps will you take to help your leadership recognize and develop their creativity?
5. Have you inventoried your God-given resources?

Perspective

Are You a Doer or a Dreamer?

Brainstorming may be the most wonderful thing in the world for you, or it may be sheer misery. "My problem is I have a very small brain," a woman told me once. "We are supposed to sit in a circle and come up with original, creative ideas, and I find my brain cells go into shock. I can't think of a thing to say. Then I feel stupid and wish I'd never come. Often I excuse myself and go and get the coffee and refreshments ready."

The woman who told me about this experience was in leadership in her women's ministry. This exacerbated her concern.

"If I'm a leader, then I *should* be able to think of creative, innovative ideas, shouldn't I?" she asked me.

"Not necessarily," I answered her. "Some do that better than others. We have dreamers among us who can dream up all sorts of wonderful things at a moment's notice, and others who have nightmares about doing so.

"By the way," I added, "how was the coffee?"

"What?" she replied, with a confused look.

"How was the coffee you went out to make?" I pursued.

"Fine, " she answered, obviously wondering why I had asked such an off-the-wall question. "That's my thing."

"Ah," I smiled, "I thought so. I can promise you there would be a woman sitting in that brainstorming circle who, in between flashes of inspired ideas, was thinking to herself, 'Oh dear, I hope they don't ask me to go and make the coffee. I never know how much to use because I'm such a klutz in the kitchen.'"

She laughed as she got the point.

I am not suggesting that we only do the things we enjoy doing, are talented at, or are spiritually gifted for. In the course of ministry there are plans and programs that leaders must plan and program, and there are practical tasks that need to be done with the same sense of high and holy calling as any other task. Many times we do not have the privilege of only doing the so-called spiritual things or practical duties that must be accomplished for a ministry. Perhaps we find ourselves with too few helpers and leaders and we must wear hats that do not naturally and easily fit. It is often in the course of filling unnatural roles that unknown gifts are discovered.

I think of my own writing skills that I was totally unaware of. As I found myself needing to multiply leaders, I appointed three helpers to facilitate small group discussions. "We can't teach," they told me. "I don't expect you to," I soothed them. "I'll draw up a worksheet to help you guide a discussion time after my lecture." "We'll try," they gallantly offered. And so we began a grand experiment together, during which one of those group facilitators found out that she could teach, and I discovered I could write!

The secret is seeing a need, being willing to serve the Lord and people, and getting going. In the course of serving, gifts we love to use will be developed, untapped talents will surface, and most important of all, the job, whatever it is, will get done!

JILL BRISCOE

Chapter 4

Put It All Together

If you are interested in developing women's ministries, you probably feel excited by the possibilities, and yet a bit over-whelmed by the responsibility of taking on such a challenging task. If you are unsure about the best way to pull a new ministry together, this chapter will help provide some of the concrete details you'll need to get your ministry off the ground.

Meadowbrook Church, an Elmbrook church-plant, serves as a good example for developing women's ministries from the ground up. Their leadership team began by putting into practice the principles outlined in chapter 2. Then they chose a fun, simple, and short special event to kick off their women's ministries. Here's how they did it.

PLANNING A KICKOFF EVENT

Two women's Bible studies had sprung up a year after Meadowbrook was planted. One was offered on Wednesdays at 6:00 AM for all women. The other met every other Tuesday morning and was specifically designed for moms. Because women from both of these Bible studies shared a concern for the needs of other women within and without the church, they decided to form an ad hoc planning committee. Using the four steps detailed

> **Choose a fun, simple, and short special event to kick off your women's ministries.**

under Planning Your Program (see p. 138) they decided on their purpose and the method by which they would accomplish it.

Their threefold purpose was:

1. To help women get to know one another in the church.
2. To find out what the women perceived to be their own needs.
3. To learn what kind of ministries these women would be motivated to attend and serve.

They chose a special event as the method for achieving their goals. During their discussion it was suggested that the event be brief, fun, and interactive.

Next they developed their program. Through prayer and brainstorming they selected the theme *Spring Planting for a Fall Harvest*, chose a morning format, specified a location and date, and listed specific means for achieving their goals for the day.

Responsibilities were delegated to everyone on the planning committee. This was easily done by listing what areas needed the oversight of a committee position. Then each person present said what they were willing to do with the Lord's strength.

Committee Positions

Coordinator(s)

Secretary

Publicity and Printing

Decorations

Refreshments

Worship

Devotional

Platform

Icebreaker

Focus Groups

Setup and Clean-up

Prayer

Audio

The committee was small, so a few women took more than one area. Everyone was encouraged to develop their own sub-committees by recruiting friends and asking for their help.

A calendar was determined outlining what must be done and by when. Publicity deadlines were set for putting together an invitation, registration flyer, bulletin announcements, and a phone-calling campaign. Planning-committee dates were set. Since they only had two months lead time, the committee met every other week until the event and planned a combined celebration and evaluation meeting for shortly after the event. A prayer calendar was assigned for the last two weeks leading up to the day so all committee members would be praying for one another, the event, and results daily during the preceding weeks.

Since the event was not covered in the budget, we minimized costs by inviting women to contribute through baking. Women signed up to bring a treat and were given the recipe. This not only cushioned the budget but also sparked enthusiasm and encouraged participation. Several of the women loved trying out the new recipes and enjoyed the opportunity to contribute to the ministry. Through increasing involvement, more women shared a sense of ownership and responsibility for the ministry.

We also asked eight women to donate door prizes. The women asked were delighted to be included and were creative in their shopping. Many of the prizes tied in to the spring planting theme, such as a watermelon salt-and-pepper set .

There was no charge for the event, but donations were encouraged by placing brightly colored children's sprinkling cans designated for Women's Ministries donations on each table. During the event it was explained that donations would be accepted to cover the cost of the building rental (Meadowbrook meets in a public middle school) and decorations. The program itself was two-and-a-half hours long, and baby-sitting was provided.

Through increasing involvement, more women shared a sense of ownership and responsibility for the ministry.

LEADING A KICKOFF EVENT

After a warm welcome and an explanation of the morning were given, the women participated in an icebreaker to mingle and introduce themselves to one another. Plenty of time was allowed for this exercise, and it gave everyone a chance to become acquainted in a relaxed and friendly atmosphere.

Sample Program

9:00	Welcome
9:05	Prayer
9:10	Icebreaker
9:25	Worship
9:35	Scripture Reading
9:40	Devotional
9:50	Special Music
9:55	Instructions and Prayer
10:00	Refreshments and Door Prizes
10:20	Worship
10:28	Prayer
10:30	Sprouting New Ideas
10:40	Focus Groups
11:25	Closing and Prayer

WORKING WITH YOUR THEME

The decor of the room grew out of our planting motif. A blue cloth, checkered paper plates, red cups, and sunflower napkins adorned each table. On the center sat two clay pots filled with dirt pudding desserts, a sunflower, and a spade. Garden gloves in primary colors lay beside the pots and the donation watering cans added a festive touch. Crates, bushels of hay and apples and baskets full of garden vegetables were scattered about the place. The entrees from recipes sent home were spread across two tables, making the room look like a market.

Time for casual interaction was intentionally built into several segments of the morning. A devotional, "Tending God's Garden," focused our thoughts on what ministries God might want to plant in our midst. Later in the day an inspiring talk entitled "Sprouting New Ideas" helped women to recognize that they all have creativity because they are made in the image of their creative God. All the activities prepared the women to imagine new and existing ministries into growth.

> **All the activities prepared the women to imagine new and existing ministries into growth.**

IMPLEMENTING FOCUS GROUPS

New women were primed for the focus groups. A trained focus-group facilitator had been assigned to each table of women.

The facilitators spent 45 minutes leading discussions that centered on the following set of questions.

At the conclusion of the group time, an assigned recorder from each table stood and briefly reported on some of the discussion in her group. The results in each group were collected to be evaluated by the ad hoc women's ministries committee.

The spring planting did indeed lead to a fall harvest. A purpose statement was determined, needs were assessed, creativity was tapped, and brainstorming was begun for a unified fall program. It was exciting to see their first brochure, hot off the press (p. 54).

FOCUS GROUP QUESTIONS

1. What is your greatest personal need right now? How would like to see yourself grow?
2. What concerns do you share for the women of our church, and is there a group of women that need immediate attention, such as widows or single moms?
3. What kinds of ministries for women would you like to see Meadowbrook offer in the future? Which would you be likely to attend or participate in? Which would you be willing to help plant (start) and grow?
4. What ministries would you not come to?
5. What ingredients are important to you in a ministry to and for women?
6. What unique needs do you think such a ministry could meet?
7. What resources do we have to meet these needs? Are they enough?
8. Will these needs last six months or six years?
9. What kind of impact would the ministries you want make on everything else Meadowbrook offers?
10. Would a new ministry be detrimental to the whole?
11. Are there any particular topics you would like addressed or speakers you would like to hear in this ministry?

MEADOWBROOK WOMEN'S MINISTRIES PRESENTS

Building Relationships:
Upward, Inward and Outward

A monthly series on Monday evenings designed for fellowship, Biblical instruction and small group interaction

7:00 p.m. Refreshments
7:15 Program

CALENDAR

September 14: BUILDING THE FOUNDATION: PERSONAL TIME WITH THE LORD at Andrea Buchanan's, 2445 N. 86th St., Wauwatosa

October 12: BUILDING A BALANCED LIFE: PRIORITIZING YOUR TIME at Beth Seversen's, 2604 N. 89th St., Wauwatosa

November 16: BUILDING THE BODY OF CHRIST: DISCOVERING YOUR SPIRITUAL GIFTS at Janet Frost's, 2456 N. 65th St., Wauwatosa

December 14: BUILDING TRADITIONS: SHARING THE MEANING OF CHRISTMAS at Adonica Randall's, 15510 Shamrock Lane, Brookfield

MORE FOR WOMEN AT MEADOWBROOK

Early Morning Study

A 6:00 a.m. weekly Bible study for every woman. Contact: Diane Sims, 744-2008

Meadowbrook Moms

A Bible study meant to spiritually encourage and refresh Moms. Meets every other Tuesday from 9:30 to 11:00 a.m. at Beth Seversen's, 2604 N. 89th St. Fall Topic: Mastering Motherhood, by Barbara Bush. Contact Kathleen Nienow, 253-0359

Women's Basket Ministry

Meals and special gifts provided for new and renewed moms and their babies. Contact Sharon Tabler, 461-3336.

Craft Ministry

October 26 Topiary Tree

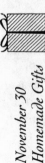

Make new friendships and create a Fall Topiary Tree of dried straw flowers and ribbon set in a terra-cotta pot. This mini-topiary is a perfect gift for a Thanksgiving hostess gift to adorn your mantel or table.

November 30
Homemade Gifts

Join together for a potpourri of gift ideas that are perfect for stuffing holiday gift basket. Many will be demonstrated and we will be making some holiday treats and take home some tasty recipes.

Contact Penny Stark, 258-1192

Birthday Party for Jesus

Hey Moms, have your kids ever been to a Birthday party for Jesus? Come celebrate with us on Saturday, December 5th. For kids ages 2 to 8 and parents, too. No gift required, He already gave.

Contact Linda Campbell, 871-9580

Part II

Meeting Women Where They Live

Chapter 5

Morning Break

Morning Break was the starting point of the Women's Ministries at Elmbrook Church. It began as a seed in Jill Briscoe's home and grew to meet in a bank, a theater, and finally in our present facility at Elmbrook, which provides for childcare and needed space. Unlike the other branches of the Elmbrook Women's Ministries, Morning Break does not target a specific group of women. Rather, it is a potpourri, a medley of women with different interests, experiences and age groups. The women in Morning Break are brought together by a common desire to learn what the Lord has to say to us through his word and to make it a part of their everyday lives. Over the years it has assumed many shapes and sizes and now offers a smorgasbord of spiritual growth opportunities.

Currently, Morning Break offers a fall format and a spring format, each with its own distinctivness. The fall program features a Bible exposition series taught by Jill Briscoe, which is followed by a choice of timely electives. The morning follows this format:

8:45–9:00 AM	Coffee Fellowship
9:15–10:00 AM	Teaching Time with Jill
10:00–10:15 AM	Break
10:15–11:30 AM	Electives or Interaction Groups

There's no better way to begin a morning than with a cup of hot coffee, a warm smile, and a friendly hello. At 9:00 AM the main session begins by welcoming newcomers with a special gift and an information packet, giving announcements, taking an offering, and joining in corporate worship.

ENCOURAGING CREATIVE INVOLVEMENT

We encourage participation in our worship through a variety of methods, including personal testimonies, songs, Scripture readings, corporate or small group prayer, skits, panels, choir, and handbell choir. A worship committee works with a theme, brainstorming and implementing ideas to involve many participants on the platform and to encourage audience involvement. One year during the fall session we highlighted a ten-minute platform segment each week entitled "Prayer Around Milwaukee." It seemed logistically impossible to take all our suburban women downtown to see what God was doing in our great city, so we brought facets of Milwaukee to them. Every week some aspect of the city was featured as a representative would briefly present their work or ministry, closing with three prayer requests. Then the representative led the women in prayer in the manner they desired: corporately, in pairs or small groups, or using open microphones. During our break between the main session and electives, the representatives were invited to set up a table presenting their work. The women were free to browse, ask questions, pick up literature, or make a contribution.

On another morning our worship committee decided to have a Fanny Crosby Day. Several of her hymns were chosen to be sung that Thursday. One woman impersonated Fanny, the famous blind hymn writer. She wore the attire of Fanny's day, and someone led her to the platform. She recited a brief personal history, acknowledging her love for God, and explained the background for one of her hymns. It's amazing how creativity flourishes when women are given freedom to put feet on their ideas!

Variety in Format Maintains Interest

Following a time of worship, Jill challenges and encourages us from God's Word. A brief break allows time for a second cup of coffee, a friendly chat, and time to get to electives or interaction groups. The interaction groups are facilitator-led groups specifically crafted to discuss Jill's message, answer questions, encourage practical applications, and support other members in prayer.

Electives are eight-week courses designed to meet women at different need levels ranging from practical to emotional to spiritual. For instance, one fall we offered three electives: "How to Help Your Child Say No to Sexual Pressure" (practical), "The

> It's amazing how creativity flourishes when women are given freedom to put feet on their ideas!

Gift of Feeling—A Fresh Look at Women, Emotions and Christian Growth" (emotional), and "An Exposition of 2 Samuel" (spiritual). Electives are designed year to year to meet the current needs and concerns of women. In years past we did not limit the number of electives. One year we actually offered a selection of twenty-two electives!

Through trial and error we learned that doing just a few things well is best. When fewer electives are offered, the leadership has a more accurate feel for what the attendees are learning and can build upon this foundation from year to year. A sampling of electives we have covered over the past few years follows:

New Testament Survey

Understanding the New Age and Other Cults

Parenting Your Adolescents

Too Busy Not to Pray

Apologetics—The Case for Christianity

Navigators I & II—Design for Discipleship

The Fact of Fiction—Literature From a Christian
  Perspective

Thread For the Needle of Life—An Overview of the Bible

II Samuel—A Man After God's Own Heart

Manuscript Bible Study of Colossians

Love that Heals—Learn How Scripture can Help us Cope
  with Chronic and Terminal Illness

Teacher Training

Counselor Training

Chemical Dependency

Chains of Blessing—For Women Married to Unbelievers

Temple Keepers—12 Step Program for Eating Disorders

Evangelism in Today's World

Choices: Moral Decision-Making at the End of the 20th
  Century

Handling Social Issues—Aids, Abortion, Euthanasia,
  Pornography

Missions in Action

Women are not required to stay for the entire morning. They are encouraged to come to the Bible-teaching time in the main session but they are free to pick and choose what they wish to attend according to their interests and schedule. We have found

Through trial and error we learned that doing just a few things well is best.

that variety keeps women's interest. Women tend to say "I've heard that before" when a program stays the same year after year. Interest and numbers tend to fall off without variety.

Interest and numbers tend to fall off without variety.

Small Groups Maintain Relationships

Our winter/spring program shifts gears to an inductive Bible study format complete with small groups. From January through May a less elaborate worship time is planned, followed by a thirty-minute lead-up to the lesson to be studied that morning. A Bible study guide is selected and used as the basis for small group discussions. The time frame for our small-group Bible study format is as follows:

8:45–9:15 AM	Coffee Fellowship
9:15–9:30 AM	Worship and Announcements
9:30–10:00 AM	Bible Instruction
10:00–10:10 AM	Move to Small Groups throughout church facility
10:10–11:15 AM	Small Group Interaction

The winter/spring format is met with great enthusiasm because it allows many women to develop and use their gifts of Bible exposition and small-group leading. It is also a highly relational time because within the small-group setting women not only learn habits of solid inductive Bible study, but they also enjoy asking questions, discussing practical life-applications, encouraging each other, praying, voicing concerns or doubts, and sharing personal struggles and triumphs. Small groups challenge individuals spiritually and provide for self-discovery of the Scriptures, an element that a lecture format alone may miss.

Small groups challenge individuals spiritually and provide for self-discovery of the Scriptures, an element that a lecture format alone may miss.

These small groups try to incorporate elements of nurture, fellowship, worship, and mission. The small groups are encouraged to take on service projects outside of Thursday mornings. Ideas are suggested from the platform, but the group is free to tailor-design their own. Here are some examples:

Working at a soup kitchen

Serving lunch to Habitat for Humanity workers

Cleaning a women's shelter

Delivering food to AIDS patients and/or their families

Volunteering time at a crisis pregnancy center or suicide hot-line

Collecting and packaging medical supplies for missionaries

Sponsoring a baby shower for an unwed mother who has
chosen to keep her child

Washing nursery toys and linens

Putting layettes together for foster parents

Sponsoring a Christmas in July for missionaries

Special events are sprinkled throughout the winter/spring
schedule in order to give teachers a break and add a dash of spice.
Special events have included a craft day when all came to make
handcrafts to be donated to our Christmas Craft Fair; a training
day on Lifestyle Evangelism; a "Preparing Your Heart for Easter"
program; and a Seminar Day that included topics such as "Caring
for Aged Parents" and "Praising in Pain" and opportunities to
learn skills like step aerobics or cooking light. One year we called
our Seminar Day "Workshops of Wisdom."

Evangelistic studies fed Morning Break and helped keep a vision for women who did not know Christ central to the ministry.

SAMPLE MORNING BREAK SEMINAR DAY

Workshops of Wisdom

You may choose two seminars in the course of the morning.

Times: 9:30–10:30 AM
             10:45–11:45 AM

Workshops of Wisdom:

. . . for the Heart
Julee will lead us in an introductory session in step-aerobics. Come dressed
to work out! (Sign-up required. Limit: fifteen people per session.)

. . . for the Family
Martha will give us some help with creative family devotions.

. . . for Grandparents
The joy of grandparenting will be shared by Carma.

. . . for the Kitchen
Susan will share some creative tricks in food preparation with three salad
treats.
(Sign-up required. Limit: 20 people per session.)

. . . for our Parents
Many of us are facing our parents aging. Mary will share from her own
experience.

. . . for our Spiritual Life
Swannie will share with us, from her own prayer life, helps to spend more
time with our Lord in prayer.

SPECIAL SESSIONS DRAW NEW WOMEN

In past years Morning Break has offered Winterim Bible studies. Instead of meeting in a main session we met only in small groups that studied a topic. Many times a committee actually wrote the curriculum; other years a Bible-study guide was used. For a time, evangelism was the focus of the Winterim studies. They met in homes throughout metropolitan Milwaukee for eight weeks. This provided the opportunity for hostesses to invite their friends and neighbors. The women who had already attended Morning Break signed up for a study at the location of their choice. One study was always held on the church premises.

Outreach was pivotal to Winterim, and several public venues like the YMCA, civic centers, theaters, and nursing homes were rented for a Bible study open to the public. After the eight weeks, Morning Break would resume its usual format on the church premises. Everyone who attended Winterim was invited to visit Morning Break. In a sense, these evangelistic studies fed Morning Break and helped keep a vision for women who did not know Christ central to the ministry.

Summerim studies were eventually renamed "Summerquest" and met at homes or on the church premises. Summerquest, our eight-week summer Bible study for women, is offered on Monday evenings and Wednesday mornings. Our summer study tends to be more topical, each week a lesson unto itself, to allow for flexibility and vacation schedules. Summerquest often draws an entirely different group of women, such as teachers and students, whose summer schedule affords them the time to attend a weekly study. Although our numbers are smaller in the summer months, we have seen lives changed and friendships cemented in this thirst-quenching program.

TEACHER TRAINING

With the enthusiasm for Morning Break Bible Study came failures and successes, problems and solutions. As more and more women joined our program, the need for more small-group leaders arose.

The Lord graciously provided leaders for electives, interaction groups, and small-group Bible studies, women who had "grown up" in our ministries. God had changed their hearts and lives, and they were enthusiastic for the Lord and his service. These women were the fruit of the Elmbrook Women's Ministries.

The problem was that although these women had a zeal and fervor for the Lord, their spiritual gifts were underdeveloped, and their doctrine was uncertain. They needed practical training on how to lead small-group Bible studies, and they needed to mature in their understanding of the Scriptures and basic Christian doctrine. Teacher Training was one of several ministries developed over the years as a solution to the increasing problem.

Each year the format and content of the course took on a different flavor depending on the class coordinator, guest lecturers, and the current needs of the women attendees.

Generally the class met every other week for two hours. This time frame seemed to best fit the schedule of "busy" women taking the course. They were able to complete their assignments when they had two weeks to do so.

The class instructor-coordinators put the syllabus together, taught the majority of the class, scheduled guest lecturers, graded all assignments, and did an exit interview with each attendee. These women who completed the course and showed promise in small group leading and in preaching to women were assimilated into ministries in need of small group leaders and teachers. Those women with inspiring testimonies were given opportunities to share them in the worship segments of our programs.

On the next page is a sample course syllabus.

ELMBROOK WOMEN'S MINISTRIES
Sample Teacher Training Syllabus

Principles of Interpretation
Building a Study Library
Using Study Tools
Sermon Preparation
    Selecting a Text
    The Subject
    The Title
    The Proposition Statement
    Classifying Sermons
    Outlining Scripture
    Creating a Teaching Outline
    Illustrations
    Transitions
    Introduction
    Conclusion
Sermon Delivery
Preparing and Giving a Testimony
Principles of Inductive Bible Study
Small Group Dynamics
Small Group Elements
Worship and Teaching

The attendees prepare and deliver a sermon, give their testimony, teach an inductive Bible study, and lead a worship session. The instructor and the classmates critique each other's presentations. A group observation guide is given to each class participant to fill out after a classmate's presentation. The course is fun and as non-threatening as possible since all the attendees must make presentations.

Teacher training has been a good solution to the problem of not knowing who all our small group leaders are and has enhanced the women's discovery and development of their spiritual gifts. Morning Break strives to reach today's women with God's word through Bible Study, interactive groups, and teacher training. We then encourage them to share their love for God and his word in their world with the hopes that they will bring others to Morning Break and to him.

Perspective

Commitment to the Same Faces

Years ago, I realized a surefire way to make certain I would grow in God. I needed to find a group of people to whom I could be accountable and for whom I could prepare some blessing. I needed to meet with them regularly. This way I was forced to forage for fresh food from the green pastures of the Word of God. This forced me to stay fresh. I knew I would need that discipline as I have a natural tendency to be lazy. Regularly planning, preparing, and preaching at Morning Break has been a priority in my life for well over twenty years. Whatever other challenges I take on around the world, I make sure I commit myself to blocks of teaching at Elmbrook.

Facing the same faces week after week means putting myself in a position of vulnerability. It means sharing who I am as well as what I have prepared to teach. After all, these people know me. If my life doesn't reflect my words, I'm in trouble. This has been very good for my soul!

There is an added bonus in sticking with one group (whatever other activities you are involved in); you share in the life cycles of other people. You get a chance to pray for their teenagers' escapades (and they for yours), rejoice at each other's weddings, and buy little rompers for your friends' baby showers. You even get to cry at each other's funerals!

Then there is the joy of watching people grow and thrive spiritually, weather catastrophe, and discover their gifts and abilities. I have had no greater joy than to convince women to believe they can do what God has assigned them to do! Fun! The greatest thrill of all is to sit at their feet and listen to their seminars and talks, marvel at their joy in serving Jesus, and become an eager pupil instead of teacher!

JILL BRISCOE

Chapter 6

Moms and More

Moms and More grew out of a Morning Break elective, beginning as a once-a-month survival training camp for mothers of young children. A handful of new moms looking for mutual encouragement gathered together and soon discovered that it was normal for babies to burp and cry and for moms to cry along with them. As the unique needs of young mothers were addressed with both biblical and practical solutions, the unsuspecting ministry began to blossom and eventually burgeoned into a thriving program reaching nearly four hundred women weekly.

Today Moms and More is described in our women's brochure as "a weekly morning ministry for mothers of young children designed to promote and encourage fellowship, Bible study, and the application of Christian principles through small-group studies, main sessions, and special programs." Moms and More didn't just happen—it began with a need, was watered by desire, and took root when willing women took a risk. From its humble beginnings a timeworn, yet liberating, principle has remained constant—in building a ministry there is freedom to fail. This concept clearly opened the back door to success.

A NEED-BASED MINISTRY

The need for some sort of support system for young mothers first surfaced at Elmbrook Church in the fall of 1977. A grandmother insightfully identified that her daughter, a mother of two

In building a ministry there is freedom to fail.

children under the age of two, was on the verge of a nervous breakdown. Overwhelmed, guilt-ridden, and tired were but a few of the symptoms she noted. Grandma, having seen the need, set out to meet it in her simple yet heartfelt way. She packed up some gifts and, armed with kind words, began to visit mothers of newborns. In time she echoed the sentiments of her daughter that "some sort of group should be put together, so these women know they are not alone."

Indeed, the idea was not theirs alone; the Spirit had been moving. Another mother, working in the Sunday nursery, noticed the haggard looks of young mothers laden with babies, bottles, bags, and Bibles. She realized that these moms could use some help.

These cries for help were soon heard by the Associate Pastor of Children's Ministries. She suggested that those experiencing the need would be best qualified for finding solutions.

So Diane, daughter of Grandma, and Bea, nursery worker, answered the challenge to get involved and agreed to team up to coordinate a brand new ministry called Young Moms. Though exact dates are unclear, the inception of Young Moms was sometime in 1978. These moms were doing well to record their children's names in baby books, not to mention recording ministry history!

The new ministry began simply, with attention given only to the bare essentials. Ten young mothers gathered once a month to pray, listen to a special speaker, join in group discussion, and share refreshments. Meetings were advertised in the church bulletin and newsletter and by word-of-mouth. Speakers were chosen from within the group or invited from outside. Refreshments and baby-sitting were handled by sign-up lists—everyone took a turn. Within a year the group had outgrown the host home and moved to the church basement. Additional hands were recruited to assist the two coordinators. These hands eventually became heads of various areas in the ministry—nursery, newsletter, secretary, and treasurer. These heads, along with the co-coordinators, formed the Planning Committee. They met occasionally in the beginning, more often as they grew. Today the committee meets once a month, and sub-committees meet independently.

Encouragement, support, and instruction marked the early years of Young Moms as women's spiritual and personal needs were met.

How Can God Meet a Mother's Needs?

In the fall of 1982 the decision was made to meet bi-monthly. The first Tuesday of the month was set aside for small-group Bible study, and the third Tuesday was designed for a speaker. This format introduced a combination of small-group interaction and large group gathering that was especially conducive to inviting neighbors.

In 1983 our purpose was transferred from hearts to paper. It drew the ministry together and directed its mission.

The Purpose
- To encourage, instruct, and provide fellowship for mothers of young children

The Goals
- To promote Christian motherhood by sharing the reality of Christ in their everyday lives through biblical instruction
- To encourage mothers, through fellowship with others, to seek God's will and to help them experience fulfillment

A purpose without a process is like building a house without a plan. Acts 2:42 provided a blueprint of ministry—teaching, fellowship, worship, and service. These events in the blueprint became, for Young Moms, the milk of the Word, the soothing ointment of fellowship, the lullaby of worship, and the pacifier of service.

A steady diet of the milk of the Word filled our mothers who were running on empty. The problem this group faced was the risk of becoming overwhelmed by all the needs of moms. . . . "I need time to myself. . . . I need more support. . . . I need more sleep. . . . I need another baby. . . . I need a better marriage. . . . I need better kids." In a small-group setting it was easy to become so focused on personal needs that God was squeezed out of the picture. The question we have continually asked ourselves is, "How can God meet a mother's needs?" That question redirects the focus. Without Christ as the focal point of the picture, no needs will be filled.

When we began to meet in small groups for Bible study, we found difficulty in gathering qualified or capable facilitators and teachers. Many mothers didn't attend because the teachers were unprepared or ill-equipped to guide the group. One mom de-

> **A purpose without a process is like building a house without a plan.**

> **"How can God meet a mother's needs?" Without Christ as the focal point of the picture, no needs will be filled.**

scribed her group as nothing more than a glorified coffee clutch. There were complaints of mothers coming and going without hearing the gospel. To correct the problem we began a required teacher training session once a month. The lessons were covered, and the teachers were equipped to interact effectively in small groups.

Planning to Strengthen Fellowship

Fellowship is essential to the effective functioning of the ministry on every level, consisting of interpersonal interaction and communication. The soothing ointment of fellowship is perhaps the easiest task to accomplish in a young moms ministry. To be honest, it's not difficult to attract mothers of young children. They are looking for any excuse to get out! After subsisting on a two-year-old communication level, adult interaction offers welcome refreshment! The only tell-tale sign of their lifestyle will be an occasional "don't touch" when you're too close to the hot coffee pot, and "no-no" when you ask if they want a cup. Though breaking back into adult company takes a little adjustment, no cost is too great to counter the intense loneliness, isolation, and frustration experienced by many mothers today.

Though coffee and cake always encouraged fellowship, old groups of friends often inadvertently crowded out the new. A shy mother recalls that she attended several months before meeting anyone. When she finally did, the mother she met said no one had ever talked to her either. A hospitality chairman was introduced to address this problem. The goal was for everyone in the ministry to be linked in a chain of care and accountability—to keep us close to one another and close to God. This chain was to spread from the newest women just entering the doors to the most deeply involved in leadership. We sought to link women together so they could support one another in Christ.

Our efforts started simply with greeting newcomers and creating special name tags for them. We sought to strengthen relationships through several channels. We increased small-group interaction and planned activities, added Shepherds (see page 77) to the small group to care for the women, used more icebreakers in small and large groups, and spent more time in question-answer sessions after speakers had finished. We also structured a care and accountability system for the entire leadership.

> The goal was for everyone in the ministry to be linked in a chain of care and accountability—to keep us close to one another and close to God.

Permeate the Ministry with Prayer and Worship

As the soft words of a mother's song lulls a baby to sleep, so the glorious sight of Almighty God is a song to our senses. Worship can flood our souls with humble admiration and praise that gives us peace and rest—the lullaby of worship. Worship is a personal prayer to God, an attitude of heart that cannot be coerced. It can be found in singing, in teaching, in fellowshipping, in serving—wherever and whenever people bow their hearts before God. Since prayer is a vehicle of worship, it must permeate the ministry. Encourage it personally, corporately, and on every level in between. Prayer and worship are the lullaby of his house; they are music to God's ear.

Challenge Women with the Satisfaction of Service

Finally, the pacifier of serving completes the blueprint. Service to a mother is a way of life at home. However, if she is not serving in the church, she will not be satisfied. A mother I knew well from Young Moms told me she was restless and needed a new project, needlepoint or something. I told her that what she really needed was to serve God. She was shocked and upset and had no idea what I meant until she tried it and found her needs were met by serving others.

PRACTICING FLEXIBILITY

We learned early on that flexibility in ministry is a key to success, and an open door to change insures progress. In keeping with this philosophy, Young Moms welcomed many changes in 1986—a name change and a format change.

Because many felt that the name "Young Moms" was narrow and made older women with young children feel uncomfortable, a contest was conducted to find a new name and logo. Moms and More was chosen as the winner and marks the ministry today.

An even more significant change came when it was decided that Moms and More should be a *weekly* ministry. The first and third Tuesdays were designated as speaker weeks and the second and fourth as Bible study weeks. Although this required increased planning and preparation time, it also created new opportunities for additional women to get involved. Women stepped out in faith and the harvest was plentiful!

> **Service to a mother is a way of life at home. However, if she is not serving in the church, she will not be satisfied.**

Moms and More exploded numerically with the new format change and by 1990 it was evident that we had outgrown our facilities. The overcrowding was actually inhibiting growth and discouraging moms from inviting friends.

Philosophically, Elmbrook has maintained that a ministry does not have the option *not* to grow. Thus another drastic change was imminent. We decided to take our biggest risk ever and literally double our efforts by offering identical Moms and More programs twice a week—Tuesday and Wednesday mornings. It was both an exciting and overwhelming decision as it required the development of two complete committees and the willingness of women to pilot what could have been a failure. However, God's grace was evident, and where he leads, he gives the results. Just two weeks into the fall of 1990, both mornings were brimming with moms, two committees were functioning at full capacity, and the enthusiasm was contagious!

The women meet in the church except for special evangelistic events. The format of the morning is the same on both days, and the program content is similar. The speaker or the Bible study material covered in small groups is the same on both Tuesday and Wednesday, although the platform time, music, testimonies, and skits may differ.

> **Philosophically, Elmbrook has maintained that a ministry does not have the option *not* to grow.**

STRUCTURING THE PROGRAM

Each spring the calendar of events is planned for the following fall. As much as possible a format is followed consisting of small-group Bible studies every other week, with special speakers or events on the weeks in between. A typical speaker-week morning might look like this:

9:00–9:30 AM	Coffee Fellowship
9:30–10:00 AM	Platform (announcements, prayer, offering, music, skits or testimonies, icebreakers)
10:00–11:00 AM	Speaker
11:00–11:15 AM	Wrapup and Closing
11:15 AM	Dismissal

Speaker weeks are designed to address pertinent topics such as "Wise and Effective Parenting," "Encouraging Spiritual Leadership in the Home," "Motherhood: The Merry-Go-Round of

Guilt," "Leading Your Child to Christ," "The Fun Side of Raising Kids," "Enhancing Marital Communication," and "Running Red Lights: Putting the Brakes on Sexual Temptation." Speaker weeks provide a gateway for newcomers, a break for teachers and shepherds, and a setting for practical learning skills and biblical exposition. Many a neighbor has been drawn into the ministry on a speaker week and eventually plugged into a small-group Bible study.

A "Bible study" morning follows this timetable:

9:00–9:30 AM	Coffee Fellowship
9:30–9:35 AM	Announcements, Offering, Prayer
9:35–9:45 AM	Music and Worship
9:45–11:15 AM	Small-group Bible Studies
11:15 AM	Dismissal

Bible study weeks offer an opportunity for in-depth study of Scripture, a time for observation, interpretation, interaction, application, and communication. Women may choose to join a small group at one of the four different levels, from a "getting grounded" group for new believers to a "digging deeper" group for those wanting a greater level of commitment.

Each small group is led by a team of two women, a teacher and a shepherd, whose collective responsibilities include leading the group discussions on the lessons prepared in the study guide and encouraging, caring for, and praying for the women in the small group, which typically consists of ten to twelve women. The teachers and shepherds are required to attend a monthly meeting and to complete the Women's Ministries' "Basics in Theology" and "Small-Group Dynamics" courses before they are allowed to lead a small group.

A Head Teacher and Head Shepherd for both Tuesday and Wednesday are responsible for coordinating the Bible-study program. They oversee and care for all of the small-group leaders and plan the monthly training meetings. Together with a co-coordinator for each day, they form the Bible Study Committee, which meets quarterly and is responsible for selecting the Bible study guide, recommending and selecting women as teachers and shepherds, and planning the program on Bible-study mornings.

Speaker weeks provide a gateway for newcomers, a break for teachers and shepherds, and a setting for practical learning skills and biblical exposition.

Bible study weeks offer an opportunity for in-depth study of Scripture, a time for observation, interpretation, interaction, application, and communication.

HELPING WOMEN MINISTER TO EACH OTHER

A unique aspect of the Moms and More ministry is our Doula Ministry, begun by the older women in the church who desired to provide a network between less experienced and more experienced mothers. Each Bible-study group has a *Doula* who sits in on the small group and is available as a resource and an encourager to the younger moms.

The Doula Ministry

In the African culture *Doula* means "the one who mothers the mother."

Purpose

To establish a network between less experienced mothers and more experienced mothers.

Biblical Base

Titus 2:3–5 NAS: "Older women likewise are to be reverent in their behavior . . . teaching what is good, that they may encourage the young women to love their husbands, to love their children, to be sensible, pure, workers at home, kind, being subject to their own husbands, that the word of God may not be dishonored."

Goal

To provide encouragement and reassurance and build confidence in the younger mother as the older mothers share biblical principles of child rearing.

Intent

It is a resource and support ministry for young moms who would like to be able to call a proxy mom with questions that perplex them.

Exclusions

The Doula Ministry is not a professional counseling ministry. It is not a babysitting service.

Caring for Children

Moms and More provides child care for children from birth to six years. Our nursery is divided by age into infants, crawlers, toddlers, twos, threes, and fours and fives. A club curriculum is purchased and utilized in the two- to five-year-old classes; toddlers are taught using a Cradle Roll curriculum. The morning is divided into play, music, Bible lesson, gym, craft, and treat time. We have discovered that a planned morning, rather than extended babysitting, is more pleasant and beneficial for the children and workers alike.

The different age-groups are staffed by paid workers and co-op moms, with at least two paid employees per area. Co-op moms presently take four turns working throughout our thirty-three week year. There is a three-dollar charge per child with a six-dollar maximum charge per family for each morning, usually paid at the time of use. A paid nursery coordinator is in charge of the paid employees and responsible for troubleshooting for both Tuesday and Wednesday mornings. A volunteer organizes and administrates the nursery co-op and sits on the Moms and More committee.

OFFERING UNIQUE EVENTS

Special events or programs are scattered throughout the fall/spring calendar. At Elmbrook these have included a Kickoff Brunch, Mission Day, Craft Day, Seminar Day, Fun Day, and End-of-the-Year-Celebration. Our Fun Day last year became our own version of *Home Improvement/Hour Magazine*. We featured mini-interviews with experts, hands-on demonstrations, audience participation, and our own humorous commercials. The topics covered included "Homemaking Management," "Quick and Healthy Snacks," "Sweatshirt Painting," "Speed Cleaning Tips," and "Teaching Spiritual Concepts to Children." The morning ended with an array of fancy and delicious hors d'oeuvres complete with sparkling cider in champagne glasses and ready-to-go recipes. Another year our Fun Day featured zany games, skits, and birthday celebrations. Tables with month markers (January–December) were decorated thematically. Women were asked to sit at the table representing their birth month and enjoyed eating a specially prepared birthday cake, sipping flavored coffees and teas, and meeting fellow birthday buddies!

PROMOTING UNITY THROUGH SHARED LEADERSHIP

Today the Moms and More committee numbers eighteen and combines the gifts and talents of many women who are responsible for various aspects of the ministry. Both committees meet monthly, administered by pairs of co-coordinators who report directly to the Women's Ministry Pastor. We have adopted a philosophy of shared leadership so that the full load of a ministry does not fall on one person and, thus, is owned by many. This has produced an environment of comradery, rather than competition, and created an attitude of excellence, rather than complacency.

Our division of leadership is outlined below. Although the number of job descriptions may appear rather overwhelming, a smaller ministry could easily adapt these responsibilities by combining several positions into one. This way a smaller committee could be sure to cover each area that is needed.

> We have adopted a philosophy of shared leadership so that the full load of a ministry does not fall on one person and, thus, is owned by many.

MOMS AND MORE COMMITTEE RESPONSIBILITIES

Coordinators

The coordinators for Moms and More are the deacons representing the ministry. They are members of the Women's Ministry Board and the Coordinator's Council. They oversee all the planning for the ministry, run the monthly committee meetings, invite and confirm all speakers, select and oversee each committee position, and work closely with the Women's Ministry Pastor in areas such as long-range calendar planning and overall vision. (See Chapter 9 for outline of the coordinators' roles and duties.)

Administrative Assistant

The Administrative Assistant will help the Bible-study team with various administrative tasks. On Bible-study mornings she will be responsible to check on proper room set up; collect, type, and distribute announcements; and maintain a count of women in attendance. She is also available for phone calling and other tasks deemed necessary by the Bible Study Committee.

Advisor

The advisor has been a coordinator in the past and remains on the Moms and More Committee to offer advice and help. She is also a member of the Women's Ministry Board.

Doula Liaison

The Doula Liaison will keep the Doulas abreast of what is going on in Moms and More, communicate the committee's vision of the Doula-Mom relationship to the Doulas, and share the Doulas' vision for the relationship, along with any questions or concerns.

Head Shepherd

The Head Shepherd is responsible for overseeing the small-group shepherds, ministering to and praying for them, and troubleshooting when necessary. She is a member of the Bible Study Committee and as such is responsible with the rest of the committee to select small-group leaders (shepherds and teachers), select the study guide used by the small groups, oversee and run the platform on Bible-study mornings, and run the monthly teacher/shepherd training meetings.

Head Teacher

The Head Teacher is responsible for overseeing the small-group teachers, ministering to and praying for them, and troubleshooting when necessary. She is a member of the Bible Study Committee and as such is responsible with the rest of the committee to select small-group leaders (teachers and shepherds), select the study guide used by the small groups, oversee and run the platform on Bible study mornings, and run the monthly teacher/shepherd training meetings.

Hospitality Coordinator

The Hospitality Coordinator is responsible for setting up and staffing the hospitality and information table on Tuesday/Wednesday mornings. She also selects and oversees greeters for any given day and keeps the Moms and More mailing list up-to-date.

Hostessing Coordinator

The Hostessing Coordinator is responsible for selecting and overseeing a committee of women to make the coffee, arrange for food, and set up and take down treat tables on Tuesday/Wednesday mornings.

Missions Liaison

The Missions Liaison plans and oversees the Moms and More program during Elmbrook's annual Missions Festival. She also coordinates the sponsorship of missionary moms by our small groups and acts as liaison between these missionaries and Moms and More. She will work closely with the church's missions liaison.

Newsletter Editor

The Newsletter Editor, through a monthly publication, keeps the women abreast of events within the Moms and More ministry and provides an opportunity for women to share information, anecdotes, prayer needs, writing talents, and helpful hints.

Nursery Liaison

The Nursery Liaison will maintain communication between Moms and More and the Children's Area Coordinator. She will also be responsible for scheduling and overseeing the nursery co-op, and for overseeing the room moms and the paid workers' appreciation coffees.

Platform Coordinator

The Platform Coordinator is responsible for platform activities on speaker mornings including physical set-up, musical presentations, testimonies, skits, prayer, and special themes. Her subcommittee may also be used as a resource for platform time during special events.

Prayer Coordinator

The Prayer Coordinator is responsible for developing and implementing opportunities to involve women in a prayer ministry for Moms and More and for individuals desiring prayer. This may include establishing prayer chains, linking prayer partners, seeking prayer support from outside Moms and More, and educating groups about prayer.

Secretary

The secretary takes minutes at the committee meetings, is available to do typing within the ministry, handles correspondence, maintains files of pertinent information, and counts and records the number of women in attendance on non-Bible-study days.

Service Projects/Social Concerns Coordinator

This coordinator will work closely with the church's Pastor of Social Concerns in selecting projects for our small groups to support that help meet the needs of various agencies in the area. She is also responsible for keeping the ministry abreast of relevant issues of social concern.

Special Days Coordinator

The Special Days Coordinator is responsible for planning and overseeing the special days scheduled for the year. These currently include Craft Day, Seminar Day, and Fun Day.

Special Events Coordinator

The Special Events Coordinator plans and oversees any special events scheduled throughout the year. Typically these will include fundraising, the Birthday Party for Jesus, and evangelistic events.

Treasurer

The Treasurer collects the offering on Tuesday/Wednesday mornings, counts it, and turns it in to the church office. She also keeps track of the Moms and More finances.

MINISTRY WITH A PURPOSE

Moms and More is Elmbrook's most need-driven, specific ministry. It is a ministry uniquely designed for mothers with young children and seeks to address the issues that accompany that stage of life that, for a time, seems bigger than life.

Many churches, small and large, have successfully begun programs for young moms because the need is so great and the concept so attractive to moms looking for an escape! In fact, a moms' program is often the place to begin women's ministries when the church has none. You can be sure that where there is a need there will be a drive to meet it. God will direct the right people to the right places at the right time.

Perhaps the testimony of a pastor's wife with four small children under the age of four will encourage you. This is from a woman in a small church in a small town with a big need:

The need is so great that a moms' program is often the place to begin women's ministries when the church has none.

As one waits anxiously for the birth of a new baby, so the women at our church awaited the birth of the M.O.M.S. program (Making Our Mothering Significant).

What a needed program M.O.M.S. is! Our purpose was to meet the needs of mothers of young children through spiritual and practical means with the ultimate goal of introducing them to Jesus Christ.

We formed a committee and divided the responsibilities. After prayer, the Lord provided a teacher, nursery worker, and helpers. We advertised on local radio stations, cable TV, and in newspapers. We made invitations and posted them at the YMCA, grocery stores, laundromats, libraries, hairdressers, the pediatric ward at the hospital. . .wherever moms hang out! The most effective way of reaching other women was through friendships—personally inviting neighbors, workmates, and friends.

Our program is geared for mothers of infants and children through school age. As the women arrive they enjoy a cup of coffee or tea and a nutritious snack. They then participate in a craft time. Fellowship and smiles come naturally. Following the craft time there is a featured speaker, video, or panel dealing with topics such as "The Winter Blahs and How To Beat 'Em," "Depression, Discipline and Your Child," "Flower Arrangements," and "Italian Cooking." We aim to incorporate both the spiritual and practical, including opportunity for discussion.

We've found that young mothers are craving to meet together for support and encouragement. With very little effort, you can start a ministry to young moms in your area that will have lasting effects.

Perspective

Quiet Times in Noisy Times

How do you hear God's voice in the midst of the mess, the muddle, and the noise? I used to have a very good talk on "The Quiet Time." That was before we had kids. After our third child was born, I gave up any attempt at getting up before them in the morning. Anyway, the noisy and hectic demands of those early hours were not a fitting environment for a quiet time with God! I soon learned I needed to create my own little closet around my soul in the middle of the mess, the muddle, and the noise.

I have often recounted the story of climbing into the children's playpen (after taking them out of it) and sitting down with my Bible and a cup of tea to a blessed daily interlude that stopped me from going crazy!

One of the saving things for me in that season of young motherhood was to discover other young moms just like me. What a relief to find out that they, too, had had a week of frustration searching for the quiet moment when they could commune with God. Perhaps it was a case of "misery loves company." I don't know, but I do know finding kindred souls was, for me, an answer to prayer.

That's what a moms' ministry is all about. Encouraging each other from a common base. Surely, finding a peer group of fellow mother pilgrims is one of God's ways of helping us to be the mothers we are intended to be. To hear a mother a little older and wiser say, "This too will pass," helps us believe it will, that this period is only a stage and will soon give place to the next set of challenges. To be able to hear a sister in Christ share a problem and pray for her means help can flow two ways. To mourn over a miscarriage together or rejoice over a safe delivery adds color and depth to all of our lives. And above all, spending time in the Word and growing up in Jesus means we will only enhance our marriage and mothering.

If you don't have a moms' ministry at church, start one in your own living room. Just invite your neighbors and friends to bring along a playpen, their kids, and the Bible, and tell them you'll provide the cup of tea. Then you're in business!

JILL BRISCOE

Chapter 7

Evening Edition

As the 1970s began, the number of women attending the Morning Break Bible Study declined. Eight hundred women was not an unusual number to have in attendance at the Bible study. However, this number slowly decreased until it dropped to half of the usual attendance. What was happening to make the women stop coming?

Soon after the decline began, an astute woman asked, "What are you going to do when your women begin to work outside of their homes and are not coming to your Bible study?" It didn't take us long to realize that this woman's question was exactly what Morning Break was facing. The trend of women returning to work had made its mark on the women's ministries.

As it turned out, God was already preparing the hearts of two women, Dell and Mary, who had a desire to minister to these working women. Dell and Mary were similarly equipped to meet the challenge. Dell managed a party-planning business. Mary was one of the top real estate brokers in the area. They had flexible schedules and understood the distinctive struggles and family pressures facing working women.

For years Morning Break had provided spiritual nourishment for Dell and Mary as well as opportunities to use their leadership gifts. Mary was inspired by a plaque that hung on a friend's wall: "If you've got the burden, you've got the job." Dell remembers being unable to find a ministry for working women that would meet her needs and muttering prophetically, "Well, I'll just have to start a study myself!"

The trend of women returning to work had made its mark on the women's ministries.

When the Lord gives us a burden to minister, he doesn't always use us immediately in the area for which he is preparing us. For years Dell felt that the Lord was calling her to help working women. She felt it the most during the year she was caring for her ill father-in-law, a time when she had to set aside most areas of ministry. During this time Dell met well-known author and speaker Evelyn Christenson, who encouraged her to pray and prepare with the admonition that when the timing was right, Dell would know it.

Then one day, just after Dell's father-in-law had moved in with another member of the family, Mary approached her to say that it was time to begin the ministry for working women. Evelyn had been right. Dell recognized it was time to begin.

Pray and prepare, and when the timing is right, you will know it.

HOW TO BEGIN

God knew it would take working women to understand other working women's needs. However, God did not call a complete committee all at once. He started with two willing women who had the abilities to form the committee, launch ideas, and instill vision in others. It was the work of the Holy Spirit that enabled, equipped, and enlightened their way.

To begin, Dell and Mary asked and answered many questions:

—"What kind of ministry are we creating?" A Bible study for women who were busy during the day and were seeking an evening alternative.

—"What will be the purpose of the study?" To minister directly to the needs of women, whether single, married or retired.

—"What will be the ministry objective?" To tell the truth about the gospel of Jesus Christ through Bible study, guest speakers, Christian artists, testimonies, fellowship, counseling, prayer, and music.

"What should be the format?" The same general style of the Morning Break Bible study, because it had proved its effectiveness:

A cheery welcome
Warm and friendly music for group singing
Announcements relevant to the women
Offertory
Musicians or vocalists to present special music
Guest speaker/artist (thirty-minute message)
Closing prayer

Developing a speaker list was important. Since Jill Briscoe's availability was limited, they recruited additional speakers. Men and women were approached who were able to relate specifically to the needs of the working woman. Asking qualified Christians to speak who were also in the marketplace was ideal, although not a definite criteria.

Topics Need to Speak to Working Women

If women were going to come to the study after a long day at work, when they had a million things left to do at home and were tired to boot, this ministry had to fill their needs and have value for them. Otherwise, they were not going to put out the effort to attend. The studies needed to meet the women where they lived. The first list of topics offered included:

Time Management
Burnout
Conflict Resolution
Job Satisfaction
Relationships
Victorious Christian Living
Values
Evangelism in the Workplace

It was amazing to see this young ministry take shape. As women were given the task, details seemed to fall into place. Both Dell and Mary were "self-starters," women who could start and finish a project with little or no supervision. The challenge of beginning the working women's ministry gave both of them extra energy, enthusiasm, and drive. In the face of challenge, both were willing to do double time to complete the task.

Realistically, two people could not do all the work. A spirit of shared responsibility needed to be fostered among the women who attended the study. This would occur as women participated in decision making, carried out different functions of the ministry, shared their new ideas, and helped implement change. Without ownership the group would have remained just "Dell and Mary's study," rather than a study for working women by working women. High on the list of things to do was the task of finding other women to help with the ministry, but first, there were basic tasks to accomplish.

> **If women were going to come to the study after a long day at work, when they had a million things left to do at home and were tired to boot, this ministry had to fill their needs and have value for them.**

> **A spirit of shared responsibility needed to be fostered among the women who attended the study.**

DOING FIRST THINGS FIRST

Deciding on the location and night of the week were the first items on the to-do list. Elmbrook Church was the easiest consideration for the location, as most of the women were familiar with the building. A meeting room large enough was available only on Monday evenings. With these two items checked off, Dell and Mary moved on to the next task.

Announcing the New Study

Obviously, women needed to know about the study so they could plan to attend. With much enthusiasm, Morning Break announced the birth of their new daughter ministry. Local newspapers were sent the good news for their community news section. This was great advertising and no cost was involved other than the time to prepare the announcement and the price of a stamp. The church bulletin printed a small announcement, and a pamphlet was distributed to women as they left church on Sunday morning. Word of mouth completed the communication circle.

Dell recalls with a chuckle that first pamphlet. Equipped with only a typewriter and press-on letters, she painstakingly sketched miniature stick women climbing up a ruler to illustrate the new ministry's name—Women on the Grow. It was a great example of using what you have where you're at. At this point, it was important to get the word out rather than to have everything perfect.

The Cornerstone Is Laid

Women on the Grow made its debut with Jill Briscoe as the guest speaker, and over fifty women attended on that memorable evening! Coffee was served, name tags distributed, and friendly greetings extended to all as they arrived. Enthusiasm abounded, and the study was off and running! The new challenge was to keep up with the pace.

THE COMMITTEE TAKES OVER

It didn't take very long to develop a team of willing workers who would become the nucleus of your structure. Some volunteered their friends, and others volunteered themselves. In the months and years ahead there were teams of hostesses, a music coordinator, a weekly newsletter editor, and a recording expert to duplicate tapes of the messages. A core of women prayed over

It was more important to get the word out than to have everything perfect.

requests that had been put in a tin can, and others went through our lay counseling program to better bear the burdens of women. There was even a "Show and Tell" person who would interview one of the women in the study each week so that all would get to know her. The dedication and commitment of these women was reflected in their attendance, completion of responsibilities, and duration of involvement. Over and over, Dell and Mary watched God fill the gaps and meet the needs of the ministry. They discovered first-hand the time-worn principle: when God calls, he equips and enables!

TRYING NEW IDEAS

In time, committee meetings proved to be launching pads for many inventive ideas, though not all of these ideas were implemented. Some ideas were tried, but didn't succeed. The ideas that worked were built upon, refined, and used often. Some of the successful ideas were:

Tell It As It Is

Sometimes a regular attendee would share a personal testimony. Other times, the women were broken into small groups and given a question or idea to discuss. Sample questions were: What did you do this weekend? Share the best meal you made this week. What is the hardest thing you experience on your job?

A Weekly Perk

As coordinator of the ministry, Dell would open each study with a warm and friendly welcome. She would present a dramatic little story, an emotional reading, or a touching poem. These special additions proved to be an inspirational highlight.

Testimony Night

Women would sign up to tell their own stories. The committee members would interview each of these women in advance. This testimony time would replace a speaker on the night's agenda.

Seder Meal

Jews for Jesus, an evangelistic ministry, presented an actual seder meal. Women were encouraged to bring their families to this valuable learning experience.

"Sip Some Soup" and "Crunch a Bunch of Salad" Nights

These nights women enjoyed fellowship over a meal. For the soup night, the participants would all bring soup, and it would be dumped into one huge pot. Astonishingly, this was truly a delicious meal. The same idea was used for the salad, with lots of different salad ingredients tossed in one big punch bowl.

The meal was served one hour before the start of the Bible study. Then a film would be shown in place of the usual speaker. Soup and salad nights proved to be the perfect opportunity to bring a friend for the first time.

Holiday Specials and Season Kickoffs

The emphasis was always placed on special music by local Christian artists. Adding a skit and inspirational reading filled in the program for the evening.

CHANGING WITH THE TIMES

Eventually Women on the Grow became Life after Work, and in 1982, Elmbrook's working women began to focus on the mission field between their own two feet—the unreached working women of Milwaukee. Targeting workplaces downtown, Brown Bag Lunch Bible Studies were developed. A contact person, someone who worked in a particular building, provided the room and publicity, while Elmbrook provided the teachers. In addition, Jill Briscoe presented evangelistic messages that shed light on life in the working world. Dinner talks were also held with the purpose of inviting non-Christian friends and co-workers. Following the outreach we offered a four-week class called "Basic Christianity." This class explored such issues as: "Is the Bible Reliable?" "Is the Resurrection True?" and "Who is Jesus?" After completing this course, attendees were encouraged to enter an existing Bible study.

Approximately four times a year we sponsored a special Saturday Breakfast Series held in local restaurants. Christian businesswomen and men, or panels, spoke on timely topics relating to work and the Christian life. Occasional outreach events provided services such as a Color Analysis or Nutrition and Diet Workshops in order to bring friends and co-workers to a more neutral setting. A salvation message was presented at these breakfasts, and the Bible study was promoted.

Most recently Life after Work has undergone a face-lift. Realizing that many working women's issues are being dealt with by companies, our women began to ask for in-depth Bible study and more personal interaction, something lacking in their high-tech, low-touch world. In response, our format has changed from addressing workplace issues to offering Bible study, with an emphasis on solid Bible teaching and small groups. The group appeals not only to working women, but also to mothers who prefer an evening study.

The year's format consists of a ten-to-thirteen-week fall series that breaks in late November, a shortened winter series of four weeks featuring Jill Briscoe, and a ten-to-thirteen-week spring series. A Bible-study guide from Serendipity House or NavPress or Zondervan forms the framework of the fall and spring series. To reflect these new changes, a new name was incorporated—Evening Edition. In our women's ministries brochure it is described as a "Monday-evening option of Bible instruction, small-group interaction, and personal encouragement for all women."

The following is the typical format for a meeting: thirty minutes of Bible instruction in a large-group setting and one hour in small groups (eight to ten women per group), including time for discussion, practical application, and prayer.

6:45–7:00	Refreshments (donated)
7:00–7:20	Icebreaker, announcements, prayer, and offering
7:20–7:25	Introduction of speaker
7:25–8:00	Introduction and exposition of passage
8:00–9:00	Small-group discussion and prayer

Because the majority of women from Evening Edition work outside the home, the focus of the ministry remains Bible study and small-group discussion time without a strong emphasis for outside ministry opportunities. As Evening Edition has grown, so also has the committee that serves it. Today the leadership group puts to use the gifts and abilities of many capable and willing women to add creativity, fun, and refreshment to an evening set aside for otherwise busy women.

Perspective

Women Wearing Many Hats

I have always worked outside of the home, as well as inside. Maybe one unusual difference between my experience and many other working women is that my work has been as a volunteer. I am a lay person, never having served on the staff of a mission or church, and yet I have run a successful pre-school with more than two hundred pupils for eight years, started, led, and developed Elmbrook women's ministry for more than fifteen years (a full-time job). I have also traveled and spoken around the globe and served on the boards of Christianity Today, Inc., and World Relief in a voluntary role. I have never charged a fee for the ministry I am asked to give, though I accept travel expenses and love offerings. Only as an author am I remunerated. I know by experience all the work and stress involved in balancing two worlds. But it's a lot of fun!

It also is a lot of work. Ministry is not a mystical thing, though there are moments. By and large, it is practical. I once made the statement, "I love everything I do," and received a letter commenting that if others could fly around the world speaking to hundreds of attentive and appreciative people, they would love it too! "What about the people who aren't successful and do all the hard work while you are up on that platform taking all the glory?" she asked me.

Perhaps that is what people think—that the thirty minutes they hear you speak comes easily for body, soul, and spirit, that there is no grunt work attached. I want to assure you there are usually hours, days, and sometimes weeks of invisible hard work, bone-aching travel, and sleepless nights before those thirty short minutes up in front of people!

Why do people think women who wear many hats do it so effortlessly? Many women don't want to have multiple responsibilities, but they have little choice in the matter. Others do not realize the added stress they'll experience when they take on a job outside family walls. Often, they find that their families do not lower their expectations of them inside of the home and yet women enjoy the fruits of their labor in the work force. This can, and often does, lead to tensions in family relationships.

The church needs to support such women—but how? If a woman has been out all day, she's not likely to be lured out again at night for a church meeting! As our ministry's awareness and concern grew for this group of women, support resources were mobilized and a structure was put into place. Personally, I identified fully with the working woman's dilemma. A ministry built on common ground, that is, gathering women together who shared common strains and stresses, gave us a flying start in establishing some help, instruction, and a framework of blessing.

JILL BRISCOE

Chapter 8

The Widow's Might

Just this noon an all-too-familiar scene was reenacted. Once again a distraught woman stopped by, engulfed in her grief and overpowered by its accompanying problems. Her husband had unexpectedly died a few weeks ago, and now the reality of the situation was crashing down around her. The funeral was over, the flowers had faded, the guests had returned to their homes, and she was alone. There were numerous decisions to be made, bills to pay, jobs to attend to, and she felt unprepared and insufficient for it all.

Nights were especially long. Every strange noise frightened her, sleep wouldn't come, and her sense of loneliness was acute. It was then that the worries and fears began. Now she was reaching out for help.

It was to meet the needs of such people that "The Widow's Might" was begun at Elmbrook Church a few years ago.

The request for such a ministry came from the widows themselves. Caught in a situation not of their own making or desire, they recognized their unique needs and presented them to one of the pastors at the church. They desired an ongoing ministry in which they could meet for fellowship, a place for the sharing of needs, understanding, Bible study, and prayer with other women who had suffered the same loss in their lives.

Following this request, the first group of widows met. Since they understood each other's needs, they were able to reach out lovingly and caringly to one another. They forged bonds of friendship, reached out to others in like circumstances, and strengthened lives so women could make necessary decisions and move on.

Jill suggested the name for this group, "The Widow's Might." When Jesus was in the temple, he saw a poor widow put her "mites" (two small copper coins) into the offering (Luke 21:1–4). Jesus commended her for putting in "more than all the others," for "she out of her poverty put in all she had to live on." The little had become much in Jesus' eyes.

Even though widows have been stripped of the one with whom they shared their lives and had dearly loved, they still find their real "might" in Christ. He becomes our strength, our guide and close companion, our supplier of daily needs, indeed our all in all. And so our focus is on Jesus Christ. He has promised that he will never leave us, but rather he is there to comfort us, to sustain us, and to be an ever-present help in time of trouble.

The group meets twice each month and is led by a retired missionary, a widow herself. It is composed of widows from several churches and denominations. Each meeting consists of a time of praise, a short Bible study, sharing of concerns, and prayer. Occasionally there is a guest speaker who comes to address some particular subject appropriate to the needs of the group. They have "adopted" a missionary to whom they write and for whom they pray.

For those women who may not have family nearby, the group goes out together monthly after church for dinner at a central restaurant. On holidays, such as Easter or Christmas, they join with one another for a special holiday dinner. These women go on short trips together to enjoy a concert, drama production, meeting, or event. Such excursions are both stimulating and fun, especially because they are shared with each other.

There is great freedom within the group to call one another on the phone when troubled or lonely, and there is always a friendly understanding person on the other end of the line.

Recently the women sponsored a special "tea" for all those living in a beautiful senior-citizen apartment complex. As they reached out to fellow widows, they shared their love and concern for them and invited them to join the meetings. The desire of those in Widows's Might is not only to be uplifted and encouraged themselves, but also to be aware of others in need and to "comfort those in any trouble with the comfort we ourselves have received from God" (2 Corinthians 1:4).

Part III

DEVELOPING YOUR LEADERS

Chapter 9

The Coordinator's Board

Partnership is a key philosophy to our Women's Ministries. In keeping with Jesus' model of sending his disciples out two-by-two, we have developed a unique women's ministry structure, our Coordinator's Board. It is made up of two representatives from each branch of our ministry. These women are known as co-coordinators and work with a committee of ten to fifteen women.

Each coordinator is hand-selected by the pastor-director of women's ministries and is asked to serve a minimum of two years. No maximum term of service is set, but it is requested that two coordinators from the same ministry (barring unforeseen circumstances) not step down in the same year to insure a balance of experience.

The Coordinator's Board is not designed as an event-planning committee, but rather as a visionary body which oversees policy and leadership. Each set of coordinators oversees an individual ministry but together they hold in trust the integrity and mission of the overall Women's Ministries.

It is required of each coordinator that she

1. Is a church member and regular attendee.
2. Models the following characteristics:

- Obedience to God and his Word
- Growing personal intimacy with God
- Devotion to ministry
- Humility
- Integrity
- Team spirit
- Receptivity
- Ability to delegate
- Vision
- Enthusiasm
- Servanthood

3. Agrees to meet once every six weeks as a team with women's pastor. This has proven to be a tremendous time of laughter, camaraderie, spiritual growth, burden-bearing, and bridge-building between varying branches of the ministry.
4. Mirrors Christ in her home and/or work arena.
5. Nurtures and develops the committee members in her charge by conducting a monthly committee meeting and staying in touch regularly. Just a note: committee members are not required to be members of Elmbrook. Many women have joined a committee and then joined the church or helped establish a vibrant ministry in another church.
6. Draws other women into leadership and encourages them to get involved.
7. Maintains an advisory capacity upon stepping aside from co-coordinator position.
8. Participates in a yearly team-building day.
9. Each year sets personal and ministry goals with pastor of Women's Ministries. During the summer months, time is set aside to assess how she met her goals. These coordinator assessments have been excellent times for friendship development, learning personal needs, and encouragement as each coordinator indeed sees ministry growth. It is also a strategic opportunity to point out areas that need improvement. And, if a particular woman in a year shows no change in a weak area, it can become the basis for a tactful dismissal if necessary. This pastor-coordinator time

provides a check for our "no maximum" time of service. A simple coordinator questionnaire follows.

Our Coordinator's Board is an active and close-knit body of women striving to meet women's needs to the glory of Jesus Christ. Our structure sets them free to minister, not just administrate. We love meeting together, serving together and together watching God work through the women he provides.

ELMBROOK WOMEN'S MINISTRIES

Coordinator Questionnaire

1. Identify the strengths and weaknesses of your ministry.
2. Where would you like your ministry to be by the end of next year in terms of:
   Spiritual Growth
   Outreach
   Equipping
   Other
3. What are you doing to meet these objectives?
4. How will you measure your progress?
5. How often do you meet as a committee?
6. Is there a body life within your committee?
7. By what means are you recruiting committee members?
8. How would you like to expand your ministry?
9. Where would you like it to be in five years' time?
10. What ministry needs can the Women's Ministries' Pastor help meet?
11. What is your one greatest personal need as you minister?
    To think about:
12. What do you do that no one else can?
13. What is the most strategic thing you personally can contribute to your ministry?

Elmbrook Women's Ministries Structure

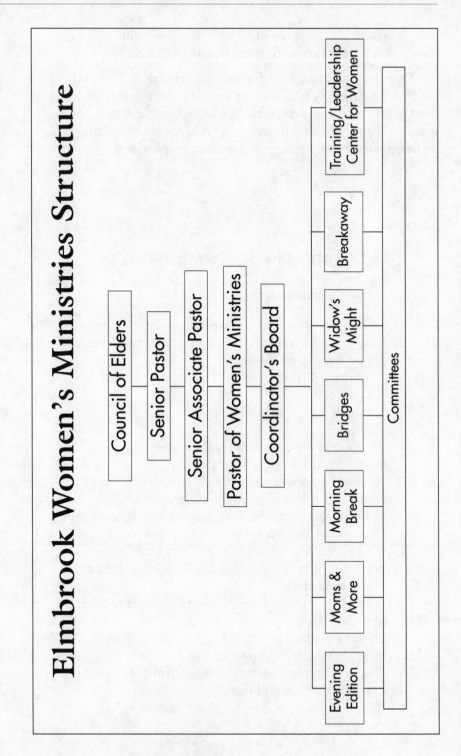

Council of Elders

Senior Pastor

Senior Associate Pastor

Pastor of Women's Ministries

Coordinator's Board

Evening Edition • Moms & More • Morning Break • Bridges • Widow's Might • Breakaway • Training/Leadership Center for Women

Committees

Chapter 10

Looking for and Leading Your Leaders

Whether you are inaugurating a brand new women's ministry, resurrecting a lifeless one, or feeding a blossoming entity, your challenge as a pastor or director will include developing and ministering to your lay leadership ranks. It seems God has created us as beings who enjoy being challenged and stretched. We are fascinated by the growing process and are attracted to knowledge, nurturance, and the honing of our abilities. We want to grow spiritually and find deeper expressions and applications of Christian truths in our lives. We long for love, acceptance, and affirmation from others and our Lord. These God-instilled needs cry out to be filled.

Despite these deep needs, leaders often suspend having their own needs met because they are so actively engaged in ministering to others. Caught up in a never-ending cycle of ministry and family responsibilities, some leaders will not naturally take the time to pause for rest, refreshment, or rejuvenation. They may not vocalize their needs or even be aware of the growing frustration, stagnancy, depression, or burn-out they may be experiencing, but the impact of a tired and emotionally or spiritually depleted leader will eventually be felt throughout the ministry.

As a women's ministry pastor or director, you have a responsibility to help guard against these dangers and care for the needs of your women. Your leaders may benefit from theological education, training in leadership, encouragement and challenge, or further opportunities for service. Others may simply need a sabbatical! All of your women will be growing at various spiritual rates, each with differing needs, hopes, and expectations.

UNDERSTANDING LEADERSHIP DEVELOPMENT

How can you help meet those needs, as well as facilitate personal and spiritual growth within your ministry? With leadership development, by which you energize and motivate your women, you can open their eyes to their spiritual gifts and help them to stretch and grow. You can train them to better lead and teach other women, which is the heart of evangelism and discipleship. Perhaps most importantly, a leadership development emphasis sends a clear message to your women. It says, "You are valuable to me and to the Lord. I care about helping you grow, and I want to invest time and resources in your development as a whole person in Christ." Leadership development is not only significant, but it is also strategic within a ministry because it provides a more equal shouldering of the work load and enhances a ministry's effectiveness in reaching its goals.

This chapter will focus on providing a fundamental understanding of leadership development, as well as offering practical programming ideas that can be uniquely tailored to your women and ministry. By incorporating solid leadership development into your ministry, you will accomplish two goals: You will (1) build up the ministry by training solid Christian leaders and (2) build up the people of your ministry by meeting the personal and spiritual growth needs of your women. As your leaders grow, they will learn how to help others grow, resulting in benefits that will resonate throughout the entire ministry.

Let's begin by defining leadership development. *Leadership development* is the expressed commitment to the lives of key individuals through strategies and programs that encourage and nurture self-esteem and spiritual growth. It seeks to foster increased satisfaction and ministry excellence, resulting in greater glory to God.

Now let's break down this definition for further understanding. *Expressed commitment* means a stated message which is understood by those involved. It is possible to have a leadership development effort in place that is silent and secretive. One could easily beef up the "thank yous" given after a job well done, or provide some casual group interaction that encourages team building, but an unspoken message always runs the risk of being unheard or totally missed. One can *act* lovingly to another, but there is something uniquely poignant about being *told,* "I love you." Leadership development is an act of loving and leading our leaders. You need to *tell* them they are loved, and then follow up that statement with actions that reinforce your commitment to them. A commitment to leadership development communicates love to the women, acknowledges them as leaders, affirms your dedication to them, and announces your desire to cultivate them. What a wonderful message it is to give and hear!

Leadership development is an expressed commitment to *the lives of key individuals.* This phrase emphasizes that human lives are involved (as opposed to mere programs), and that human needs will be addressed. In our self-absorbed society, the idea of meeting human needs might be met with some disdain in a religious context: Aren't we supposed to be focused on God? Of course that is a valid question, but God has created us as humans with needs—social, spiritual, relational, physical—the very heart of which is our need for him. Jesus Christ instructed us to care for human needs and personal spiritual development. "What you do for the least of these, you do for me." When we intervene in the lives of others in a way that increases their love for God and potential for serving him, we are fulfilling what he has called us to do.

Our efforts must be directed toward *key individuals,* leaders. Some people have difficulty acknowledging they are leaders. At Elmbrook, we have occasionally refrained from using the term "leadership" when titling special events, because the very mention of the word intimidates some women—even those already in leadership roles! But however you describe your leadership development effort, it must be narrowly focused toward the group of individuals who are either currently involved in a leadership function or who would profit greatly by such preparation.

Leadership development is an act of loving and leading our leaders.

Leadership development is accomplished *through strategies and programs.* The most thorough and effective leadership development is planned, purposeful, and programmatic. Planning insures that your leadership development is well-contemplated and structured. It has a purpose that is understood, and it is established as a program. The word program does not mean that each aspect of leadership development must be an event, but rather the process itself is a recognizable whole, designed to be an integral part of your ministry schedule and priorities.

The goal of leadership development is to *encourage and nurture positive self and spiritual growth.* Although the intent of leadership development is to focus on the women themselves, by far the most successful results will occur when the spotlight is placed on Christ. Leadership development is not self-centered, it is Christ-centered. When women are taught their true identity in Christ, the struggles with "self" are lessened. As women's talents and gifts are identified and nurtured, they begin to discover their God-endowed potential. Understanding the power available through God's Spirit allows women to worship and serve God in the fullness of who he created them to be.

> Our definition of leadership development seeks to foster increased satisfaction and ministry excellence, resulting in greater glory to God.

Lastly, our definition of leadership development *seeks to foster increased satisfaction and ministry excellence, resulting in greater glory to God.* It is only natural to expect that as women grow to be more godly and proficient in serving, they will be more deeply satisfied personally and experience greater excellence in their church leadership roles. As women learn how to model their own lives after the leadership style Christ presented, ministry to the church and the world is enhanced, giving increased glory to God.

Jesus' Model

Experience has shown that leadership development brings an exciting return for the investment, but the most compelling reason for making it a part of your ministry is that Jesus modeled it. Jesus knew that he would use men and women to be his Good News messengers, so from the beginning he chose and cultivated a team of leaders. Though his disciples numbered twelve men, his intimate circle also included key women. These women learned from him, participated in his ministry, and even supported his efforts through their own financial resources. These discipled women were so well versed in theological truths, that the Easter morning proclamation was entrusted to them.

Though people flocked to him at every turn, Jesus frequently took retreats with his ministry team away from the crowds. In a haven of peace and quiet, Jesus taught them and explained parables. He ministered to their needs and fears and taught them to trust. He comforted and strengthened them and filled their hearts with hope. He provided experiences that would stretch and challenge them, preparing them for future responsibilities. He modeled leadership with the perfect balance of authority and servanthood.

SETTING OBJECTIVES FOR DEVELOPING SOLID LEADERS

Leadership development is both practical and biblical. It develops both the beginner and the veteran. In building a strategy for leadership development suited to your particular ministry, begin by identifying several key objectives, since these will form the foundation for your programs. Here are five for your consideration:

- Involve your women
- Inspire your women
- Instruct your women
- Instill passion and commitment in your women
- Intercede for your women

Involve

The starting place of leadership development is the selection of leaders. Simply *asking* women to be involved begins the leadership development process. Many potential leaders have remained in the background, too shy or unsure of themselves to come forward and volunteer to lead. As an administrator, you have an ongoing task of identifying possible leaders and facilitating their involvement. As you begin, keep in mind several key principles for recruitment:

1. *Start small*—Don't be overwhelmed by the task of immediately filling every possible ministry position that comes to mind. It is all right to begin with a skeleton committee, or a few hand-picked women. At Elmbrook we have

Simply *asking* women to be involved begins the leadership development process.

found it is much better to have a few good, qualified teachers, than an extensive roster of unprepared, illsuited workers.

2. *Look in unusual places*—One woman was discovered serving coffee in the kitchen. When it was noted that she was faithful in little things, much more was entrusted to her. As leaders, we must help women reach new personal ministry heights. While it would have been comfortable, perhaps even natural, to leave Mary Ann in the kitchen, giving her additional responsibilities proved mutually beneficial. She eventually became a co-coordinator of Morning Break.

3. *Have job descriptions*—When possible, provide women with an explanation of what is expected in advance. Help someone say "yes" to a potential ministry role by spelling out such specifics as time commitment, responsibilities, and job parameters. A complete job description lessens the possibility of the disappointment and frustration which ambiguity causes. The flip side is that a job description may encourage an entrepreneurial spirit to exclaim, "Oh I can do this—in fact, I can do *more* than this!"

4. *Consider the concept of "mom-sized" jobs*—Many women want to be involved in serving, but due to certain seasons of life may have limitations. In order to help them create a healthy balance of work, family, and ministry, we have taken several committee positions and divided them into more manageable "mom-sized" jobs. For instance, in the past our hospitality coordinator was responsible for greeting newcomers, helping them find a small group, and making follow-up phone calls. A once overwhelming committee position was easily split into three more inviting, mom-sized jobs. Now three women serve in the capacity of one.

5. *Be in the business of helping women find their niche*—This means encouraging women to discover their spiritual giftedness and helping them get placed in that area of service. Recently we asked a willing woman to serve as a small-group shepherd, a task requiring mercy gifts. As the year progressed she became increasingly discontent in her position, critical of her small-group leader, and performed

poorly as a shepherd. Feeling completely inadequate, she wanted to quit, and we frankly almost encouraged it. Upon reconsideration, we realized that perhaps her position simply did not match her gift mix, and at heart she was most likely a teacher. The following year she returned in a new capacity and proved to be an outstanding small-group leader. Lesson learned.

With these key principles in mind, you are ready to begin recruiting. Women want to serve, so don't be shy about asking! Here are some suggestions and methods for conducting the recruitment process:

- *Asking for volunteers*—Send out a message that help is needed and see who answers the call.
- *Shoulder-tapping*—This one-on-one contact allows you to hand pick leaders and is an especially effective method for filling key leadership roles.
- *Nomination*—Ask the women you work with who might be best for a particular leadership position; their answers might surprise you.
- *Co-coordination*—As explained in chapter 9, at Elmbrook we use pairs of women as co-coordinators in the top levels of our leadership. This allows more women to be in leadership, and creates strong ministry duos which share workloads and provide encouragement, challenge, and support to one another. As "iron sharpens iron," women mature as co-leaders of ministries. The co-coordinator approach helps train new women leaders through a transfer of ministry experience, allowing a comfortable transition into leadership, since full responsibility is not shouldered by one person. All of our ministry coordinators are asked to make a minimum two-year commitment (we currently do not have a maximum term) to the ministry in which they serve. In addition, both coordinators are asked not to step down from their leadership position within the same year, creating a balance of experience.
- *Cross-over leaders*—A ministry can grow leaps and bounds when a leader working in one area is asked to bring her talents and experience to a new area. As she is challenged in

new ways (a great cure for stagnancy), the ministry also benefits from her fresh insights.

- *Partnership surveys*—At the end of each year, women are asked to complete a partnership survey, indicating their gift areas and interests in serving. The surveys are kept on file and are a helpful resource when ministry opportunities arise (see sample in appendix 2).

A sure-fire way to stifle ministry growth and dampen enthusiasm in your women is by clinging too closely to every detail and responsibility.

Two additional recommendations will assist in your search for leaders. First, you are not in the recruiting process alone when you help other women develop a recruiter's eye. Encourage your leaders to be additional eyes and ears, listening and looking for women who are potential leaders. In the absence of healthy recruitment, burnout results, frustration sets in, and ministries stagnate.

Second, control your controlling tendencies. A sure-fire way to stifle ministry growth and dampen enthusiasm in your women is by clinging too closely to every detail and responsibility. You need to let go and let your women lead. And they, in turn, need to let others experiment, experience, and energetically enter into leadership.

The very nature of the word *involve* presupposes a currently uninvolved person. Although there is safety in asking the same person who chaired a particular event to do so again, why not stretch your women, take a risk, and provide a leadership opportunity for a new woman? Ask someone else!

Involve your women.

Inspire

Being a visionary means seeing the overarching plan of God and helping others grasp its magnitude.

Your role as a leader is to pass on the vision for what can and should take place in ministry. The more responsibility your leaders assume in the ministry and its dreams, the more devoted they will be to seeing those dreams become a reality. That vision must be communicated and caught by your leaders. On an ongoing basis you need to share with them your insights, struggles, plans, hopes, prayer concerns, and long-range expectations. Fill them with the truth of God's awesome strength, power, and possibilities. Welcome their ideas and encourage their excitement and progress. Being a visionary means seeing the overarching plan of God and helping others grasp its magnitude.

The other part of vision involves the day-to-day specific ideas that make a ministry work and facilitate the fulfillment of your ministry purpose statement. How do you make a distant dream become a working reality? How can you effectively communicate it to others and get it off the ground? We would like to share with you the story of how one creative concept took three years to come to life.

Two of our most enterprising women came up with a super idea. They suggested we sponsor a family-oriented fun day called "Wild, Wild West Day" (WWWD). WWWD would be sponsored by all branches of the women's ministries and include children's games (ages two to twelve), food, entertainment, petting zoo, and more. Each small group would be asked to create and oversee a game booth or help with refreshments, decorations, or clean-up.

We loved the idea, and using the following principles for communicating a vision submitted it to the entire women's ministries.

- *Tie your vision to a specific need*—For a long time our women's ministries recognized the necessity for (1) more neighborhood evangelism, (2) a heart for serving the ministry that served them, and (3) finances for increasing child-care services. WWWD provided an opportunity to invite the community into our church, let our women serve, and raise monetary funds for our child-care area.
- *Gather opinions on the "how"*—We began to ask others who had participated in similar events what they had learned and how we should proceed. We also held a brainstorming meeting to discuss various planning details—the sky was the limit.
- *Discover objections and iron them out*—We initially asked each small group to create their own game booth. But many groups were stumped and asked that the planning committee give them options from which to choose. Another objection arose over the timing. We announced the idea for WWWD in January with hopes of hosting it in May. "Not enough time," women told us, and flatly refused to help in this endeavor. So we decided to postpone WWWD, re-announcing plans for WWWD the following September and distributing a list of game booth options to each small group. Our sensitivity to these obstacles really paid off when WWWD was met with great enthusiasm the second time around.

- *Enthusiastically promote your idea*—Genuine excitement about your idea will be contagious. To aid in recruitment we utilized clever skits, colorful posters, punny announcements, fun work days, and word-of-mouth publicity through coordinators, teachers, and shepherds. Perhaps the best publicity is to do it once and let the good news travel!
- *Don't stop praying*—Several months in advance we asked our women's prayer chain to begin praying for WWWD. The head committee devoted a part of each meeting to prayer. We put the vision in the church prayer bulletin, prayed for it in regular staff meetings, asked prayer coverage by the men's ministries, and encouraged each small group to pray consistently for this event.
- *Be appreciative of your women*—All along the planning stages we thanked the women for their hard work, without which WWWD would never have happened.

Although WWWD turned out to be an incredibly successful and well-received event, not every vision is destined for greatness. Perhaps these additional principles are worth considering:

- *Don't eliminate a good idea for the wrong reasons.* Before you reject a solid plan, ask these questions:

  Is it a poor idea, or was it just poorly communicated?
  Did you target the wrong audience with the right program?
  Are the lack of resources causing a lack of enthusiasm?
  Were too few people involved to accomplish the plan?
  Was your program covered in prayer?
  Is it worth trying again?

- Experiment with a pilot program. Begin with a framework of an event and test its effectiveness and response. You may be considering a mom's program, a career women's Bible study, or a Saturday breakfast series. Before investing significant time and resources, why not try a four week trial run and ask those who participated to evaluate it.
- *Model it yourself*—If you think your ministry needs to be more friendly to newcomers, ask yourself "Am I friendly to

newcomers?" Set an example by living out the convictions of your vision.

- *Be patient.* Some ideas take time to catch on. If you impart a vision and enthusiasm is not garnered, wait. In the right time (it may take weeks, months or even years), in the right place, a seed of a vision may be cultivated into excellence with the Gardener's touch!

Inspire your women.

Instruct

It's easy to forget that shepherds are also sheep. Loaded down with responsibilities, teaching assignments, event-planning schedules and more, sometimes the concept of reinforcing our leaders' own level of biblical knowledge and spiritual growth gets forgotten. We assume they are learning as they are studying—and often they are—but this cannot replace the deeper instruction needed for ongoing enrichment. Leaders need to be learners too. First and foremost, encourage their attendance at weekly worship services. No leader should be so busy that corporate worship is neglected. In addition, provide learning opportunities for them. (See ideas below.)

Most importantly, model God's truth in your own life. A "Recipe for a Good Sermon," found in a cherished cookbook, says it well:

I would rather see a sermon
Then hear one any day.
I'd rather have you walk with me
Than merely show the way.
The eye's a better pupil, and
More willing than the ear.
Fine counsel is confusing, but
Examples are always clear.
I can soon learn to do it,
If you'll let me see it done.
I can see your hands in action
But your tongue goes on the run.
All the lectures you deliver
May be fine and good and true,
But I'd rather get my lessons

Leaders need to be learners too.

By observing what you do.
For I may misunderstand you
And the high advice you give
But there's no misunderstanding
How you act, and how you live.

—AUTHOR UNKNOWN

Our women need to see the truth lived out by us, or we are like a noisy gong, a clanging cymbal. A leader's life must exhibit the Word of God as it influences and undergirds our lives. God said it this way in Isaiah 66:2: "But to this one I will look, to him who is humble and contrite of spirit and who trembles at My word" (NASB). May we best teach others by visually illustrating these words with our lives.

Instruct your women.

Instill

As pastors and administrators we have a duty to pass on to other women a passion and commitment for God and his work by planting deep within them biblical values through meditation on God's word. Strengthen your women's understanding of the ministry by frequently communicating your goals. Help them develop their own insight for what God can do in and through their lives. In addition, instill in your leaders a sense of team spirit and oneness in Christ. Leaders obtain comfort and strength by knowing that they function as part of a team, locally in your church or ministry and corporately in the Body of Christ. When women sense this team spirit, they are more able to share the pressures and enjoy the pleasures of ministry. Divisions are diminished, and unity is strengthened. Lastly, instill in them the concept of leadership transfer by encouraging and assisting them to raise up future leaders who will carry on the task.

Instill passion and commitment in your women.

Intercede

The most valuable and important role you can provide for your women is as a prayer intercessor. This fact is known, perhaps even to an extent believed, yet is often not practiced with daily obedience and faithfulness. Why is it easier to talk about praying than to pray? Perhaps we have not learned the joy of communing with God in this way. Maybe we have not taken the time to foster the discipline. Or, quite possibly, we have become confident in our own abilities and strength. But God's power is unleashed through prayer! We are sorely irresponsible in our positions as leaders if we are not actively interceding for our flock and teaching them to pray for one another and the ministry. By making prayer a priority, we practice the trust in God that we preach. In quiet moments with him, lift up to him the ministry and women that belong to him. In this way we also teach our leaders the value and importance of personal prayer.

Intercede for your women.

These objectives are only a few of many you may want to consider as you create a leadership development program that is right for your group. Why not gather a small group of key leaders to brainstorm the needs of your ministry leaders and develop a list appropriate to those needs? Then with clear objectives in mind, you can move ahead to begin applying programs and approaches to create effective leadership development in your church.

STRATEGIES FOR YOUR MINISTRY

Mentoring

One easy way to develop leaders is through one-on-one partnering. Mentoring programs can be a very effective means of strengthening two members of a team, both the leader and follower. Pairing up older and younger women is recommended because it is both biblical and smart. The wisdom of the years is often passed over in favor of homogeneous couplings, but there is much to be valued in maturity. At Elmbrook we pair women through our Doula ministry. Each one of our small groups has a doula, and many women have special relationships with these older women. Whether someone is chronologically older or simply has more years in the Lord is less important than the overall concept. The point is to put together two women who are at differing stages in their Christian walks.

You may want to personally mentor some of your key leaders by establishing special prayer times, ministry planning days, or special times together for growth. If your organization is a large one, consider grouping together three or four leaders for team mentoring.

We are sorely irresponsible in our positions as leaders if we are not actively interceding for our flock and teaching them to pray for one another and the ministry.

Mentoring programs can be a very effective means of strengthening two members of a team, both the leader and follower.

Prayer Partners

An expansion of the mentoring idea is the prayer partnership, implemented so that women will intercede for one another. You may wish to add to this idea by developing a theme for the year or choosing a section of Scripture for meditation, but the thrust of prayer partnerships is mutual accountability and openness to the Lord through prayer.

Encouraging

It is amazing how a brief note or quick phone call can bring encouragement to one's day. You can make that difference in your leaders' lives by inexpensive, thoughtful touches. Remember their anniversaries or birthdays with a card; call them before a job interview to say you are with them in prayer; photocopy an article of interest for them; follow up after they have finished a project to ask how it went; or drop them a note just to say you love them. Especially in the face of failure, fear, pain, or disappointment, be there to bind up the bruises, hold a hand, breathe a prayer, and give a word of encouragement.

Secret Sisters

This idea combines the prayer partner and encouragement strategies. Pair up each leader randomly and anonymously with another and instruct them to encourage and pray for their "secret" sister in the Lord. Set a leadership development focus for prayers and encouragment.

Bible Studies

An indispensable method for strengthening a sense of unity, building team leadership skills, and fostering personal growth, Bible studies can provide solid teaching at levels appropriate to leaders. The Serendipity series is particularly good at breaking down interpersonal barriers and engendering good discussion. You may want to start with a topical study on leadership in Scripture, work through a book of the Bible, or choose a new book on leadership (or a theme appropriate to your leaders) that is challenging and thought-provoking. Focus on the group time together, rather than overloading your leaders with individual study preparation.

Reading Assignments

How about occasionally assigning a good book to your leaders? Open their minds to a current thought-at-large and ask for their feedback. Even short questions at the end of each chapter (or the entire book) can function to broaden your leaders' base of knowledge and insight. Suggested queries might be: "What did you learn about God through this chapter, and what did you learn about yourself?" or "How could our ministry benefit from this idea, and how would you implement it?" or "What did you find personally challenging about this book, and how can I encourage you in that right now?"

Reviews and Updates

Staying in touch with your leaders and learning about their needs will help you best meet those needs and guide your leaders' growth. Schedule quarterly meetings (over a meal is nice) to get together and share. You may want to prepare an evaluation form which can be discussed at the meeting. This form might contain such questions as:

Staying in touch with your leaders and learning about their needs will help you best meet those needs and guide your leaders' growth.

1. What are the key needs of your ministry right now?
2. What are your personal and ministry goals for the next quarter?
3. What was the most successful aspect of the last ministry project your group completed? What was the greatest disappointment?
4. How am I doing as your supervisor? What do you need me to do differently?

Ask for and expect honesty if you trust your leaders and are truly interested in facilitating their growth, your own growth, and creating excellence in ministry. These scheduled review sessions do not eliminate the need for ongoing review, challenge, and communication between you and your leaders, but are useful for more focused interaction. Plan to spend several hours together discussing the ministry and their personal lives and needs. These special times of togetherness can go far in creating a solid bond between you and your leaders.

Entertainment

All of us need to put work aside at times and just have fun. Some of the most valuable leadership development will occur when you are not looking. Get your leaders together for a special outing (movie, dinner, or a game night at someone's house). You do not need to enforce a "no business" rule, simply keep in mind that the goal is to have fun, be together, and show them you care.

EDUCATING YOUR LEADERS

Mini-Institutes

We have previously mentioned the need for training leaders through education. A mini-institute can provide that instruction with minimal effort. Bringing in a guest speaker (pastor, business owner, community leader, counselor, professor) can lighten your load and offer a new perspective to your women.

At Elmbrook we have started a Training and Leadership Center for Women (TLC). Convinced that women must be biblically grounded and equipped to instruct others, we identified three key areas of leadership development that could be enhanced through the inception of a TLC:

- Training in theological truths
- Specific leadership instruction
- Personal spiritual development

To meet that challenge, TLC was created to equip, encourage, and enrich current and potential leaders. Although it is open to the community, TLC was specifically designed for the women who lead and teach our Bible studies. Offered two or three times per year, it resembles a graduate or continuing education program, with high-level, specific training concentrated into a short period of time. The TLC program takes place on a Friday evening and all day Saturday and contains two main tracks:

Track I—Basics of Theology
Suggested Prerequisite: None
Basics of Theology will ground women in the fundamental tenets of Christianity by addressing important issues such as the reliability of Scripture, the sovereignty of God, sin and salvation, the doctrine of the Trinity, and eschatology.

Track II—Small-Group Dynamics

Suggested Prerequisite: Track I

Small-Group Dynamics will help women become effective small-group leaders, developing skills necessary to start and continue a successful small-group study. Topics to be covered include How to Develop Effective Questions, How to Use Study Tools in Small-Group Preparation, Evaluation and Trouble Shooting, and Implementing Prayer Within the Small Group.

All of our leaders are required to take these two main tracks (women have up to two years in which to complete this requirement), and we require a passing grade on the "basics" exam. Once these core requirements are completed, leaders are expected to annually complete an elective designed to provide ongoing enrichment and personal skill enhancement. For example:

Track III—Biblical Responses to Life's Struggles

Suggested Prerequisite: Tracks I and II

While trials and tribulations are a part of life, God has a purpose for all of them and has promised that a believer in Christ can be an overcomer in every situation. In his Word, God has given us everything we need to live in a manner that pleases him. This elective is designed to help you apply God's word to difficult circumstances in your own life and the lives of others and understand its timeless truths for today.

Christian Apologetics: A Ready Defense of Your Faith

This track will help in understanding and responding to some of the major questions people in the '90's ask about the Christian faith. It offers historical and biblical evidence for Christianity addressing such issues as how we know the Bible is true, Jesus— truly the Son of God, creation vs. evolution, the question of evil and suffering, and more.

"Titus II"

The "Titus II" track, open to women of all ages, will help women develop the confidence and skills necessary to be an encourager or mentor to other women. The four sessions will define mentoring and help you in your preparation to respond to a request to mentor. The sessions are designed to give you skills needed not only to begin, but to continue such a relationship.

Our TLC teaching staff is made up of pastors, women in the church, and local experts. For instance, the teachers for Small-Group Dynamics include an elementary school teacher with Campus Crusade experience and lesson planning skills, a pastor who can explain how to set up and use a personal study library, a man who has extensive experience leading small-group Bible studies, and a woman known in our church as a sincere prayer warrior.

Because leadership training is essential to effective ministry, it is offered at no cost. Printing costs are absorbed by the women's ministries budget, and attendees are asked to bring a bag lunch. Binders for notes were donated by local businesses, and we used the church facilities and classrooms.

Our TLC program has attracted hundreds of women and has proved rewarding both to the individuals and our ministry. The women feel better prepared to be leaders, and we have gained increased confidence in their leadership abilities as well. Laying solid biblical foundations, strengthening women spiritually, and providing a contagious learning environment have provided a deep pool of trained leaders from which we fish.

Conferences/Seminars

Another significant learning option is to send leaders to outside conferences or seminars. Many reputable parachurch organizations offer excellent training for leaders, including Walk Through the Bible, Christians for Biblical Equality, Campus Crusade, and Leighton Ford Ministries. Encouraging your leaders to attend other church events can also be helpful and invigorating. They will undoubtedly obtain new ideas and perhaps a deeper appreciation for how your church or organization operates.

Graduate Education

Christian colleges and seminaries frequently offer classes that are beneficial to lay leaders. Many offer courses which are available through satellite locations or via correspondence. Consider asking a professor or seminarian to come to your church and present a class. A free-will offering, sponsorship by a business, or tuition fee could help defray expenses.

Additional Opportunities

Ropes Course

Many Christian camps offer a two-tiered, team-building exercise called a "ropes course." Groups can participate in either high-level (off the ground) or low-level (on the ground) courses. Both provide a fun, interesting, and educational way for your leaders to learn about themselves and each other. At a ropes course the instructor creates scenarios in which problem solving is required and teamwork is challenged. For example, our group of twelve women was shown a small wooden platform that represented a "rock" in the ocean. We were told that our (imaginary) ship was sinking fast, and our challenge was to quickly save all twelve on that rock. Active conversation, strategizing, and negotiating ensued as we worked together to complete this task, and a sense of encouragement and satisfaction arose when we achieved our goal. We found that personality differences, leadership styles, fears, and expectations become acutely pronounced when faced with some of the challenges. Taking a team on a ropes course is a great way to strengthen an existing team or nurture a new one. Be prepared to learn about yourself in the process!

Leadership Retreat

Pulling your leaders away from familiar surroundings to focus on spiritual things is a fabulous investment in their lives. Plan to host a leadership retreat every one-to-two years, limited to your leaders. (See chapter 11 for a detailed presentation on creating effective leadership retreats.)

Leadership Conference

Different from the leadership retreat, the leadership conference has a more general focus on equipping and enriching women in and for leadership. It can take place at or away from the church site. It is open to the community, providing a resource for other churches, and guest speakers are sometimes invited for the plenary sessions. Although a leadership conference involves more work than some of the ideas previously listed, *you can do one*, and its leadership development benefits are excellent.

The most important aspect of hosting a leadership conference is creating an attractive, inspiring, and challenging program. We have found the greatest success in developing different goals for

Pulling your leaders away from familiar surroundings to focus on spiritual things is a fabulous investment in their lives.

each day of the conference. Here is a brief outline of what was presented each day:

Thursday Evening—Emphasis on Encouraging
Welcome / Icebreaker
Worship
Guest Speaker—Opening session
Receptions—(1) General, (2) Ministry wives

Friday—Emphasis on Equipping
Worship
Guest Speaker—Plenary session
Seminars
Lunch
Seminars
Guest Speaker—Plenary session

Saturday—Emphasis on Enriching
Worship
Extended platform program (including drama and
        special music)
Guest Speaker—Plenary session
Early Lunch
Seminars (two sets)
Guest Speaker—Plenary session

PROVIDING MINISTRY EXPERIENCE FOR LEADERS

Leaders need more than education; they also need a challenge. A specific challenge offers them an opportunity to take a risk and to trust the Lord. Over the years the Elmbrook Women's Ministries has developed a Speaker's Resource Guide. Somewhat like a speakers' bureau, the guide categorizes women according to their gifts. Keynote speakers, Bible teachers, seminar leaders, worship leaders, and consultants are listed. Under each category are several women's names, with addresses, photographs, and brief biographical sketches including the topics they address.

As women hone their craft through TLC Leadership Conference, small-group leadership, and committee work, they are also encouraged to develop their speaking gifts by leading a seminar or teaching an introductory Bible lesson within Elmbrook Women's Ministries. After their gifts are confirmed, they are encouraged to take engagements outside the church, and if their speaking gift continues to be recognized by many, they are added to the Speaker's Resource Guide.

We chuckle when we refer to our "experts." Our experts are merely ordinary women making themselves available to our extraordinary God and accepting any challenge he presents to them, including speaking opportunities.

BUILDING YOUR LEADERSHIP RANKS

As you raise up and develop leaders, here are several important concepts to keep in mind:

1. *Recruit*—Continue to add new leaders to the leadership ranks and increase your group of potential leaders.
2. *Regroup*—Form teams among your leaders and occasionally change these teams for new relationships to form.
3. *Respect*—Learn about varying leadership styles and the need to understand and celebrate differences.
4. *Recognize*—Be generous with hugs, encouraging notes, verbal praise, zany awards, and any other fun ways to say thank you to your leaders.
5. *Reflect*—On an ongoing basis utilize focus groups, surveys, and one-on-one review sessions to facilitate greater growth and mutual understanding of what is good, lacking, and what could be improved upon. Listen more than you speak during these times.

These are only some of the many ideas you may want to try as you establish a leadership development effort that will best meet the needs of your women and ministry. If you are feeling overwhelmed, simply tailor our program to your particular audience. Sometimes we avoid trying new things because we have never done it before. Fear of failure and time commitments can paralyze our thoughts and stifle our creative energies long before we have given the idea a chance to prove its worth. Why not sit down with a group of your leaders and brainstorm the possibilities? Prayer will help you determine what kind of leadership development is right for your group.

Though it may not always seem outwardly apparent, our leaders need special nourishment and care. The following story illustrates this truth.

> **Though it may not always seem outwardly apparent, our leaders need special nourishment and care.**

Two beautiful yellow canaries were perched in their cage, singing sweetly the whole day through. Life was nearly perfect. Their owner, a kind man, fed them and gave them fresh water daily. He talked to them and even tried to chirp and sing along. It wasn't canary-perfect, but they appreciated his thoughtful effort anyway. One day the man had to go on a business trip. Fortunately, his roommate would be home to care for the canaries.

Every day at the break of dawn when the light came pouring into the kitchen, the canaries began to sing. The roommate would awaken and smile. Those sweet, yellow canaries, he thought. They really sing beautifully. The roommate went about his daily life, smiling every time he thought about the canaries. Every time he passed their cage he smiled, and the canaries sang and sang.

Three days later the kind man returned home. To his horror he discovered his beloved canaries dead, lying on the bottom of their cage.

Frantically the kind man found his roommate and asked, "My canaries are dead. Do you think it was something they ate?" Suddenly the roommate's face turned white. Food, he thought, food and water. Every day he heard their singing as he walked past their cage. They looked so beautiful, so happy, just fine. How could he have forgotten to feed them?

Chapter 11

Effective Leadership Retreats

Imagine this scenario. Your ministries are active and growing. Your people are being nurtured and challenged. But your leaders are getting tapped out and tired. What is the solution? Perhaps it is a leadership retreat, a time to pull together the group of women who are dedicated daily to the task of planning and executing creative programs for women, but are sorely in need of personal refreshment and revitalization for themselves. A leadership retreat can offer a needed reprieve to devoted workers while paving the way for even more productive and life-changing ministry ahead. This chapter will explore the benefits of conducting a leadership retreat, providing you with creative ideas and guidelines for planning your own.

WHY A LEADERSHIP RETREAT?

First, let's consider the philosophy behind hosting a leadership retreat. We know that rest is an important part of life, but our busy lifestyles demonstrate that we seldom take this fact seriously. Between raising children, preserving a marriage, pursuing a career, maintaining a home, doing ministry, and growing in our relationship with God, we rarely have time—or take time—to simply relax and enjoy life. The phrase "stop and smell the roses" seems somewhat outmoded. Who has time to *stop* these days?

A quick scan of a concordance shows that the word *rest* is used frequently in Scripture. Though it can refer to God's perfect and eternal rest planned for us in heaven, it also pertains to physical rest from our daily labors. The rhythm of life that God has established for us contains an ongoing ebb and flow of work and rest.

We can take our lead from Jesus in this matter. When the rigors of daily ministry began to take their toll, Jesus spoke to his key disciples saying, "'Come with me by yourselves to a quiet place and get some rest.' So they went away by themselves in a boat to a solitary place" (Mark 6:31–32). He took his leaders away from the group at large and gave them needed time for fellowship alone with him and with each other.

Rest also relates to our need to trust in Christ's work on the cross. Salvation is accomplished for us through Jesus, and we *rest* in this. In addition, God has promised to finish what he has begun in and through us. The burden is not ours. As much as we enjoy throwing ourselves and our energies into ministry, we must remember that God is the designer and finisher of his plan. Resting, therefore, shows our trust and enjoyment in knowing that God is in control of it all.

A leadership retreat provides leaders the time and permission to relax. It offers a healthy focus on the need and benefits of physical rest and spiritual rest in Christ. Rest is a key component of a leadership retreat, but it may not be the sole motivator. Perhaps you have goals such as strengthening the friendships that bind your leaders together, training and equipping them for new or increased service, planning future strategies for ministry, or deepening their personal devotional lives through a retreat of prayer and worship. Depending on your own leaders' needs and desires, a leadership retreat can take many shapes. We will provide some general suggestions as well as profile one of our recent leadership retreats.

Deciding on a Goal

The first step in planning an effective leadership retreat is to determine the purpose. What do we need to accomplish or want our women to gain? Possible answers might be—

> **A leadership retreat provides leaders the time and permission to relax.**

- An opportunity to relax and have fun
- Personal spiritual growth through study
- Quiet time with God
- A time to regroup, reflect, and evaluate
- Goal setting, focus time, or planning ahead
- Group nurturance, building unity and team spirit

This list is obviously not exhaustive. By polling a few key leaders you may get a pulse for what is most important for your group at this time. You may want to combine several goals to create a retreat that will best suit your leaders' needs. Be cautious not to pack in too much though. A retreat that is too busy will defeat its purpose, and no one (including you) will have any time to rest!

After determining the goal, you will want to decide on a theme. A theme provides the framework from which every other aspect begins to take form. Find a key Bible verse which captures the goal and theme you have in mind. Here are two illustrations of how it works:

Your Goal

Provide group nurturance and assurance of God's love for the individual

Key Verse

"The unfolding of Your words give light. . . ." (Psalm 119:130)

Theme

Unfolding His Love—For You!

Ideas

The invitations are cleverly folded and sealed like a love letter

Bible teaching is done in stages, gradually "unfolding" the truths

An icebreaker involves speed in folding and unfolding towels

A craft time includes origami (paper folding)

Folded notes are placed, with a candy heart, under the pillows of overnight guests

Your Goal

Equipping, goal-setting, and motivating for a specific ministry task ahead

Key Verse

"You did not choose me, but I chose you and appointed you to go and bear fruit—fruit that will last" (John 15:16)

Theme

Harvesting Forever Fruit

Ideas

Nametags are shaped like different fruits

Prank—A luscious tray of caramel covered apples includes one caramel covered onion!

A farmer gives testimony about dependence on God to bring forth the harvest

Individual workshops are entitled:

Refreshing Rains of Rejoicing (praise and worship)
Sowing Super Servants (how to lead others)
Cultivating Caring Communication (relating in relationships)
Yielding to Him (servanthood and selflessness)

Notice how the theme permeates the entire event. A theme verse helps establish focus for your retreat and provides fertile soil for great planning ideas.

In planning a recent leadership retreat at Elmbrook, we sat down to discuss the needs of our leaders and the desired goal of the retreat. Because we have so many women in leadership, we wanted to bring a deeper sense of unity to the women involved in our various ministries, and a sense of togetherness in serving God through his plan. We sought to provide personal spiritual refreshment and team unity in a fun environment. With that in mind, several theme ideas were developed for consideration.

The key Bible verse we decided on was 1 Thessalonians 5:24, "The One who has called you is faithful, and *He* will do it!" (paraphrase, emphasis added). We felt this verse incorporated both God's choosing and empowering of leaders. The promise of

> **A theme verse helps establish focus for your retreat and provides fertile soil for great planning ideas.**

that verse made our theme selection quite easy. We called it "Mission: *Possible*," since every mission is possible when God plans and empowers it. With this theme we stressed how each leader was involved in God's mission, regardless of where she individually served, enabling us to foster increased unity among women in our ministries.

Your key verse and theme set the tone for the rest of your planning. Now you are ready for the next step.

Selecting a Site

As you begin to envision your retreat, it is time to shop for the perfect location. What will best fit your theme, meet your budget demands, suitably accommodate your guests, and provide the ideal setting for achieving your goal? Typically, a local hotel or a Christian camp come to mind when planning a retreat, but why not be creative here too? How about—

- A bed and breakfast, or rentable landmark mansion (Minneapolis has several)
- A farmhouse or barn acclimated to accept groups (Mooove your group away from the city hype!)
- An inner city community center (Perfect for combining a weekend outreach with your retreat.)
- A park or forest preserve (Good for a one-day event and cookout.)
- A local YMCA or health club (Combine spiritual and physical aerobics for a day of getting totally fit!)

We selected a Christian retreat center that doubles as a housing and recreation facility for the handicapped (Inspiration Center, Walworth, Wisconsin). It had an excellent, large meeting area, an adjacent chapel, plentiful motel-like rooms and cabins, a kitchen with full-time staff, and a swimming pool, all set in a woodsy location.

Brainstorming Bonanza

Once you have some idea of the theme and location, it is time to have the first major brainstorming session. For the basic principles and guidelines for brainstorming, see chapter 3.

A brainstorming idea worksheet can be very helpful. Provide categories or subheadings that need to be thought through and discussed. For example:

- List basic information about the retreat (dates, location, theme, goal)
- Give a preliminary agenda with times and events planned (if ready)
- Offer a list of key phrases playing off the theme from which to expand (e.g., spy, clues, alias, hideout)
- List specific items that needed brainstorming (games, teaching time, skits, worship)

Decide in advance what ground you want to cover at this brainstorming meeting. Do you want to establish a final schedule, develop a brochure or invitation, or simply lay a creative foundation? Coming into a brainstorming meeting prepared with some initial ideas and a goal will make your work as a coordinator easier and less frustrating. Depending on the scope of your event, one or several brainstorming sessions may be necessary. Then after laying a creative base, you can begin to build the planning committee.

Building a Leadership Retreat Committee

Perhaps committees get a bad rap because they often spend too much time figuring out what they are supposed to be doing. Without solid direction, a committee can easily wander in a wilderness of frustration or inertia. A good coordinator is generally someone who is organized and can engender the dedication of others.

When recruiting women to work on a committee, strive to achieve a balance of gifts and talents. Know where your own shortcomings lie. One of our coordinators loves to brainstorm and work details down to the last decorative degree, but she dislikes accounting functions and is admittedly terrible at making anything crafty. When building a committee, therefore, she deliberately selects women who can do what she can't. The tendency is to find people just like ourselves, but when we do, we find that all the things we are terrible at end up being done terribly! Although you will need people who share your visionary skill

When recruiting women to work on a committee, strive to achieve a balance of gifts and talents.

and creative knack, the committee (and the event) will suffer greatly if diverse abilities aren't used.

We had a coordinator working full-time on "Mission: *Possible*," and several brainstormers also agreed to help plan. More committee members were recruited, generally to help oversee specific activities (invitations, registration, skits) as they arose. A separate decorations committee was added later. A total of twenty women and less than six committee meetings brought "Mission: *Possible*" from start to completion within two months.

Record Keeping

The benefits of a good filing system are tremendous! It is easy to forget, the details especially, when things are happening rapidly. Saving scraps of paper where you've jotted down an innovative idea, that phone number of a bakery willing to make a possible donation, or the names of women contacted who would like to help next year but can't this year, will not only come in handy in the future, but will help you keep your sanity and details in order in the present. One expandable file folder and just a few labeled files can do the trick. Hint: Set it up early so you can use it throughout the planning process.

WHOM TO INVITE AND HOW

Perhaps you already have in mind the persons who would most benefit from a leadership retreat. We had more than three hundred! Obviously some work had to be done to narrow down the list. Since one of our main goals was unity, the larger the number of guests, the more difficult closeness and unity would be to achieve. We wanted women from our various ministries to get to know one another better—not simply hang out with those they already knew. So we trimmed our list down to only those leaders, teachers, and coordinators who were going to be in active leadership that fall. A few others were added who showed great leadership potential, in order to help them grow toward future ministry positions.

Our leaders, like many of yours, get asked to participate in any number of things. Brochures of upcoming events are always tempting them to attend. We wanted them to view "Mission: *Possible*" as a unique event planned especially for them, so we first made personal phone calls to every woman we wanted to attend.

This accomplished three things: it cut down on our mailing costs, because we later only sent invitations to those who expressed an interest; it allowed us to introduce our theme through these "secret" phone calls; and, third, the women were excited and flattered to be asked in this one-on-one fashion, causing anticipation to grow for the event. In the end, approximately 125 women attended our retreat.

Work hard to make the written invitation introduce your theme idea. Use graphics or clip art in an original way. Play with the text to develop puns or wording that will grab attention. Here is an excerpt from the opening lines of the "Mission: *Possible*" invitation:

> **URGENT COMMUNIQUE . . .** The phone rings. She answers it. The voice is low, summoning, authoritative. The 24-hour mission will convene at a remote vista. Few are called. Fewer are chosen. She accepts the call.

In addition to the who, what, where, when, and why information that is necessary, it will be helpful to include a list of any items the guests should bring, and a map and directions to the site location. Consider whether you want your leaders to choose their own roommates (if your retreat is an overnight one), or if you will strategically assign rooms in order to develop new friendships. Include the cost (if any) of the event and what the price includes (meals, materials, lodging). If possible, offer partial or full scholarships for women in financial need.

Our invitation required each participant to pay for the retreat in advance, which is especially helpful if you have a large group, and to give themselves a "secret agent" name. We used these secret agent names throughout the retreat and had great fun with them. Even after our retreat some women continued to address others by their aliases.

A WORKABLE TIMETABLE

Planning a special event takes time. In order to squeeze in all the elements you would like to include, work with a reasonable timetable and achievable deadlines. If you have ever glanced at a wedding magazine, you will notice that it always contains a timeline of what needs to be completed by certain benchmark dates. The timetable actually works backward from the day of the event to the present, helping you envision what must happen by when.

It's funny, but in some ways a large wedding is no different from a small one. One must still consider obtaining the dress, the cake, the flowers, the guest list, the music, and . . . the groom! Although a big wedding costs more, it can take just as much time to plan a small one. A retreat works the same way. Obviously, if yours is very elaborate, it will take more time to plan—but you will be surprised how much time is involved in planning even a relatively simple event. Creating a workable timetable helps you stay on track, serving as a reminder for each task.

FASHIONING IT TO BE FUN

By working in just a few goofy games, an innocent prank or an energizing crowd breaker, you can make your event go from satisfying to super. We literally spent hours reviewing game books, talking with youth leaders (it is quite amazing what kids will do), shopping and scavenging for props, and testing out possible ideas. It was well worth it. Here are some tips we discovered along the way:

Icebreakers

The purpose of an icebreaker is to make guests feel comfortable and begin shifting their attention from real life to retreat life. It can be light or serious, but should involve some interaction, either verbally or through the completion of a task. For "Mission: *Possible*," our opening icebreaker served several functions. It developed the theme, divided the group into teams, and provided interaction.

We found clip art pictures of spy or mystery-related subjects (e.g., a woman peering into an old mansion, a top-secret suitcase) and had them blown up into poster size, one poster per team. The posters were then glued onto cardboard and cut into puzzle pieces (the number of puzzle pieces matched the number of women on a team). Each person was given a puzzle piece in their packet of materials when they arrived. Their first "mission assignment" was to find the other members of their team by putting together a completed puzzle picture. An original copy of each picture was mounted on the walls of our main meeting room and served as both decoration and a visual reference of the completed puzzle.

> **The purpose of an icebreaker is to make guests feel comfortable and begin shifting their attention from real life to retreat life.**

Games

Games are especially good for building team unity.

(1) Try combining several game ideas for a new twist. We made a marathon relay out of several games that would have been so-so on their own but were incredible when merged. We called it "The Mother of All Relays."

(2) Remember the age and health of your participants. Will the older women feel comfortable doing your game, or can it be modified to make it more appropriate? Will chairs be available, or must they sit on the floor? Consider options and restrictions of the location.

(3) Run the idea of your game or specialty element past several others. This will help weed out what won't work for the masses. It may also surprise you. Our coordinator mentioned to the committee a game idea that she didn't personally like. The committee loved it, however, and it turned out to be a big hit!

(4) Try out your game idea first. What sounds hilarious might not be so funny in reality. Does it work? Will people be able to do it? How long will it really take to do? And is it fun?!

(5) It is helpful to write out the instructions for a game in advance. Simple steps can be explained from the front, but more complicated ones should be provided to guests in writing. Make sure whoever leads the game knows how it works and can explain it to others.

Games are especially good for building team unity. You can easily modify an existing game for a group setting. Try nominating team representatives to play a round of Twister. Or break into teams and play Pictionary. Make up your own Pictionary phrases for greater difficulty and more fun. Imagine ten different teams trying to draw items like these:

- Two women carrying a porcupine
- The inside of a Twinkie
- Giraffes playing leap-frog
- A pepperoni and mushroom pizza

Inexpensive prizes, crafts, or gag gifts can go far in adding to the fun of a game. Solicit a children's Sunday school class in advance to make up some creative prizes. Or ask several local businesses to make prize donations. If you can get over the fear of asking, you will be quite amazed at how willing others are to give.

Pranks

We did an outrageous prank that is worth repeating. Send someone out of the room. Set up the room with two long tables put together, but leave a one-foot gap between them. Cover the tables with long cloths to the floor. Place five different-sized boxes upside down on the tables, with one in the center just over the gap. Under four boxes place a ball (soccer, baseball, any kind will do). Under the center box, have someone kneel, so that their head is hidden under the box. They must not be seen from the front. Number the boxes 1–5, with 5 as the center box. Some distance from the tables, place a container (a laundry basket will work) in which all four balls will fit.

Bring the person back into the room. Tell her that this is a relay race against the clock. The goal is to pick up each box in order, get the ball underneath, and run to put it in the container. If she can do it within thirty seconds, she will win a prize. What she doesn't know is that when she lifts box 5, a head will be waiting!

We broke our group into teams and conducted this prank ten times, videotaping each volunteer. It was a riot. We're waiting to hear from America's Funniest Home Videos . . .

Drama

Drama can be an incredibly dynamic form of communication. Even if your group is not comprised of Broadway stars, you can effectively use drama. We did three dramatic pieces that could easily be adapted to a variety of scenarios.

(1) *TV/Movie Spin-Offs*—Because "Mission: *Possible*" was our theme, it was natural to enact a modification of the old *Mission: Impossible* TV show. In fact, we began our retreat program with a sketch using original music (available on CD), slides of special agents (key leaders), and a piece of dry ice that smoked as the tape "self-destructed." An old black dress and shoes from a thrift store helped create an inexpensive secret agent genre. Is there a movie, documentary, or TV show that could be adapted to your theme?

Drama can be an incredibly dynamic form of communication.

(2) *Song Spin-Offs*—Someone in our group remembered an old 1960s song called "Secret Agent Man." With some creative new lyrics, this became a new hit at our retreat. No one need be an opera star to carry it off. In fact, if you print up the lyrics everyone can join in the fun!

(3) *Direct-a-Drama*—One of the easiest ways to have a drama is to create a fun script that comes to life for the first time at the performance. You will need to begin with a certain plot in mind ("Missionary quite unexpectedly gets tickets to Academy Awards"), but the actors add their own spice to the drama. The script is written with certain actions that are continually changing, such as: "Then she carefully moved across the room . . . on tip toe . . . backwards." The volunteer actresses are chosen right before the performance, given props, and then set on stage to enact whatever the director reads. With effective pauses at the ellipses, this can be very funny because the actress begins doing the action one way, and then must modify it each time a new direction is given. We created a spy mystery to play off our theme. Choose your biggest hams as actresses, and you've set the stage for fun.

GETTING THE MOST OUT OF YOUR SITE

Depending on where you host your retreat and the theme you want to develop, you will need to give some thought to the best use of your facilities. Here are some preliminary categories for consideration:

The Staff

It is important to develop a positive working relationship with the staff of your facility. As the coordinator, keep in mind that you represent not only yourself, but every woman in your group and your church or parachurch organization as well. Most importantly, you represent Christ. In the midst of negotiation, disagreements may occur. Keeping a balanced perspective (hey, this is only one event in the entire scope of human history) and your eyes firmly placed on Christ will help keep your emotions under control and your mouth shut during stretching circumstances!

The facilities staff can be invaluable in helping plan your event, since they know their own site best. They are usually extremely willing to meet even the most eccentric needs. By discussing with them your individual requirements and ideas, you may find some helpful aid in working out logistical details *and* suggestions for how to do something even better. At our retreat we couldn't bear knowing that a swimming pool was available without using it, so we planned a late night pizza and pool party. The Inspiration Center staff was glad to accommodate this unusual request, even suggesting homemade pizza by their chef. It was fabulous!

Speaking of menu selection, this is a decision best made with fork in hand. Ideally, take a committee member or two to the site in advance and partake of their culinary crafts. Notice especially the portion sizes and fat content. Typically, women eat less than men and appreciate a less starchy, healthy meal. Increase the number of fruits, vegetables, and salads for greater satisfaction.

Decide in advance if you will need support staffing (if it is available) at your event. Is there an on-call person in case of emergency? Who will open and lock up the facilities each day? Can someone help with setup and tear-down? Discuss your needs in detail with the staff and enjoy not only good results but the blessing of new acquaintances.

Decorations

Add impact to your theme with decorations. Much more than simple balloons or streamers, decorations can go far in creating a whole new look or feel in your site location, as well as getting your leaders in the mood for fun. Consider the following when planning decorations:

- Evaluate each room your group will be meeting in—look at the walls, the ceiling, the floor, and the doors. What can be done to each to make it reflect your theme idea?
- Give some thought to the lodging. What can you put under the pillows, beneath the beds, in the covers, or on the mirrors which might be fun or add to the overall mood? We called the rooms "hideouts" and pretended that each was bugged by putting fake microphones in various places. We put clues in the room that led toward prizes. Secret agent snacks (a decorated bag with goodies)

were put on each woman's pillow, and the "hideouts" were given names such as "The Parlor," "The Oak Library," and "The Butler's Pantry." Each listed the occupants by their secret agent names.

- What can you do to make registration fun and different? In an attempt to create a spy atmosphere, our registration area was made to look like a safehouse checkpoint. An old gooseneck lamp and ancient typewriter adorned the table, and all the registration hostesses wore black visor caps. Some wore more elaborate 1940s period costuming or trench coats. Walkie talkies were used inside and out to announce agent guests as they arrived. Invisible ink was used to stamp registrants' hands, and a black light revealed its secret imprint.

Multimedia

If you plan on using a slide projector, screen, microphones, lighting, compact disc player, or other multimedia equipment, be sure to let the facility know in advance of your intentions, even if you plan to bring your own equipment. You may discover that the facility is already equipped with what you need, or that it is unable to accommodate your equipment. Again, your communication with the staff can serve to circumvent frustrations and disappointments and ease the planning process.

Signs

Even if your invitation contained a map and directions to the site location, it is a good idea to post signs at the site, letting your guests know that they have found their destination. If possible, affix additional signs at strategic points en route to the site to increase excitement and help point the way to fun.

KEEPING PRAYER A PRIORITY

As you plan your leadership retreat, it is easy to let the brainstorming and other work fill every waking moment. It is challenging and demanding to oversee every detail and know that thirsty leaders will be relying on you and your committee to bring needed refreshment to their lives. You will want every part of this event to bring them closer to one another and to God. Ironically, there is a danger that the planning process itself will depict the

> Your communication with the staff can serve to circumvent frustrations and disappointments and ease the planning process.

complete opposite. We've heard horror stories about coordinators running around half-crazed, barking out orders, and caring very little about the people involved, let alone God. What had gone wrong?

Obviously, the focus had become blurred and suddenly the goal and purpose had been lost amid the technicalities of the task. Perhaps more fundamentally, the ministry work had become a substitute for God himself. Our first priority must be our relationship with him and commitment to prayer and studying his Word. Carving out a portion of each day to worship him, discuss the details of the planning with him, and lift up the needs of women and the goals of the retreat are not only good ideas, they are crucial. If you want a retreat that will powerfully impact the hearts and minds of your women and foster life-changing future ministry, plan to pray daily for these things. Covering your leaders and the retreat with prayer can do what even the most creative planning and decorations cannot: It can fill your retreat with God's spirit and your women with his power.

Our leadership retreat coordinator tells the story of how, even late into the night, she would get new ideas for how to make "Mission: *Possible*" better. Then one night something pivotal happened. She awoke from a bad dream quite alert, and for some reason became immediately concerned about the need to establish a small group that would wrap this event in prayer. It was as if God woke her up to remind us of the necessity and magnitude of that need. Although we were individually praying for the retreat, we knew then that we needed others to be in deep prayer.

That next morning she contacted four women who were to share a cabin together at the retreat and asked them if they would be a prayer coalition. It was important to choose women who would be in close proximity at the retreat so they could readily meet for prayer, and if a specific need arose at the retreat, we would know where to find them. These four women prayed faithfully. On two occasions prayer sessions were held via conference call so that those with small children could participate from their homes.

We are convinced that prayer powerfully affected "Mission: *Possible*" in ways that cannot be realized, but there were tangible results as well. Our women grew closer through this event, and this retreat gained the reputation of being one of the best leadership retreats we have ever had.

PLANNING THE PROGRAM:
TIMING, PLACEMENT, AND EMPHASIS

By now your brainstorming or leadership committee has likely solidified at least some of the ideas for your program. You may have developed several games, chosen a speaker, planned drama, and slotted time for worship. This is the time for nailing down a final schedule of the events and determining what needs to go where on the agenda. As you consider the time needed for each element and exactly which elements to choose, filter your ideas once again through the grid of your ultimate goal. If your goal is largely to build relationships, you will need more items that allow for intimate communication and sharing. If your goal is strategy planning, this will take a significantly longer time than playing a game or two. Think about what you want to emphasize, and structure your agenda accordingly.

As you contemplate placement of the program elements, think of creating a flow. Just like ocean waves that get stronger as they reach the shore and then crash in a stirring crescendo, a program needs to have elements that differ in intensity. You will want your program to build to a climax at times. Perhaps it will be a teaching segment or a time of worship. You can enhance these climactic moments by grouping the other elements strategically toward that goal. For instance, if you want a time of personal sharing, you will need to lead up to it with several elements that break down self-consciousness and build up group sensitivity. An icebreaker, moving drama, testimony, or worship time can be used well here. If your goal is a strategic planning session, then perhaps a teaching time and team-building game would be an effective lead-in. Think, what is the *feel* of this session? What is my motivation and goal, and how can this best be expressed? Then, use the elements in tandem to develop the feel that you want and move closer to the goal.

At "Mission: *Possible*," we considered each half-day (Friday night, Saturday morning, and Saturday afternoon) individually and asked the question, "What do we want to accomplish during this time?" On Friday night, for example, we needed to do several things:

> **Just like ocean waves that get stronger as they reach the shore and then crash in a stirring crescendo, a program needs to have elements that differ in intensity. You will want your program to build to a climax at times.**

(1) Make the women feel comfortable and special and create a mood for fun

(2) Develop a trust between the women and facilitate a time of personal sharing

(3) Have our first teaching session

(4) Finish the evening off with fun and fellowship

A definite flow of fun-serious-fun was in mind as we put together the schedule. Here is how we compile our agenda to accomplish these goals:

Goal	Method
Make the women feel comfortable and special and create a mood for fun	Fun "spy" registration, snacks, opening drama to explain theme further
Develop a trust between the women and facilitate a time of personal sharing	Icebreaker; games, "Clues to Your Life"
Have our first teaching session	Teaching: "Clue #1 . . ."
Finish the evening off with fun and fellowship	Neighbor nudge, pool and pizza party

It would have been uncomfortable for the women to arrive and immediately move into a time of personal sharing. By allowing some fellowship time, an icebreaker, and games, they were able to relax and open up about themselves without feeling pushed.

THE GUESTS ARRIVE

The day has arrived, and you are ready for the real leadership retreat to culminate all the weeks of planning. How will the guests perceive this event when they walk through that door, and how will you make them feel welcome?

The decor will go far in creating the mood you desire, but don't forget the human element. It is people that you are appealing to, and people who are involved at every angle. Will your committee (or another they have designated) be available to greet them? Will you have refreshments available? What kind of conference materials have you prepared? Will the kickoff activity provide a transition to the rest of the retreat?

Perhaps the most important thing for you to do is to lead by example: *Relax!* The work has been done. All of your (and the committee's) efforts have gone toward this moment. Now it is time to enjoy and let God take charge! You have been involved in his plan, and he will bring it to its completion. There comes a point where you must say, "This is yours, Lord. It always has been. It's been great to work on it. Now, please, use it to your glory!"

Making It Memorable

The more you allow yourself to think about your retreat, the better planned it will be. That is what we discovered with "Mission: *Possible.*" We tried to envision the guests arriving, work through games in our heads, consider different decorations, and find new spy terminology for the retreat materials. These mental exercises were invaluable in getting the bugs out of ideas and troubleshooting possible problems.

The retreat will be memorable when new friendships grow as a result. Help these new friendships take root by distributing a guest list that includes each attendee's address and phone number so women can stay in touch after the retreat. Well-designed conference materials can serve as encouraging reminders of a key weekend as well.

MISSION ACCOMPLISHED

The joy in planning a leadership retreat comes in knowing that you not only created memories, but you offered something special to the women who serve most diligently in the ministry. You said "thank you" to them—and also to God for raising up these dedicated women.

Gauging a retreat's effectiveness and success can be done in several ways:

- Listen attentively and openly to unsolicited comments. Even if you disagree with the appraisals, respond in love and articulate your appreciation for the honesty shown. Write down the comments and ponder them carefully before casting any judgment upon their worth.
- Utilize an opinion survey. Distribute the survey to all participants at the last main gathering. Make it short, so as to facilitate the widest response, but also direct.

> The joy in planning a leadership retreat comes in knowing that you not only created memories, but you offered something special to the women who serve most diligently in the ministry.

- Organize a recap meeting of your committee members. Strive to obtain their unbiased feedback as well as any comments they have heard from others.
- Personally evaluate it. Did *you* enjoy it? Did you feel it was worthwhile and that it achieved its goal?

"The sooner the better" is the key motto for all of these approaches. Memories are fresher directly after they are made. Again, be careful not to react, but consider each comment thoughtfully.

The best litmus test for a leadership retreat's success, though, may be slow in coming. Months later, when you see your leaders involved in ministry, and they are vibrant and excited about what they are doing, you can smile and remember a certain event that provided a needed respite for weary workers. Or you might witness the Holy Spirit at work in someone's life in a way you never could have dreamed before. It may even be your own! Somewhere down the road when things begin to get a little too hectic again, a thought will come . . . "What we need right now is a good leadership retreat."

Part IV

Reaching
Your
World

Chapter 12

Breakaway for Renewal

Imagine one incredible event that includes all of the following: one thousand women dining together in an elegant ballroom, an entire room filled with suitcases piled to the ceiling, midnight aerobics, a Christian bookstore for your perusal, twenty-four-hour free counseling, skits, door prizes, music, drama, an all-night hospitality room stocked with munchies, and an abundance of seminars. Here's a few more hints: it's a sleep-over with no bed-making or dishes to wash, a safe place to bring a friend where she can hear about the Lord's love and plan for her life, and a time of spiritual reflection and growth for you. What could it be?

You guessed it! It's a Breakaway.

Our winter Breakaway at Elmbrook Church has become a tradition for many Milwaukee women. An enormous slumber party, it is held at a sophisticated hotel. Its two-fold purpose is to share the gospel with the non-Christian while providing spiritual enrichment for the Christian. This mid-winter break offers women a few days' rest from their responsibilities. The demands and expectations placed on women can be overwhelming, and Breakaway offers them a fresh perspective on life, new and deeper friendships, the opportunity to bring a friend to Christ, and best of all, a time for personal spiritual renewal.

THE HISTORY AND FLAVOR OF BREAKAWAY

Neither rain nor sleet nor snow could keep them away! After twenty-four hours with no electricity in many Milwaukee suburbs, the committee felt that we should cancel our first Breakaway retreat. Rain had turned to ice in the unpredictable March temperatures, and electrical lines were sagging and breaking beneath the weight of alternating rain and freeze. Trees were stooping to the ground with many losing branches, snapping over wires and roads. Jane, the coordinator, felt strongly that canceling the long awaited first overnight retreat would only complicate matters. She was right! Of the four hundred women registered, only twenty-five were unable to make it. One senior citizen claimed that she slid down her icy driveway on her suitcase to meet her ride! The consensus among the attendees was that they were happy to have a shower after being without electricity!

Women from a two-hundred-mile radius left home and family for inspiration, recreation, and relaxation. This was appropriately called the first annual "Women's Winter Breakaway." The year was 1976 and except for a handful of denominational retreats, we knew of nothing else in the area that offered women a chance to hear biblical truths, enjoy learning the latest crafts, see a fashion or home decorating update, engage in a game of tennis, and relax in a pool or spa. Twenty-four hours was maximized as women fondly reunited with family members and friends for an all night "pajama party." Pairs or small groups of women found lounging corners and bedrooms conducive to lengthy discussions on God's plan for the contemporary woman, his will, pressing personal circumstances, and current women's issues.

The atmosphere and program were carefully planned by a committee that met regularly for eight months prior to the event. Attendees were served and cared for in a variety of ways. Time for personal prayer, counseling, and follow-up were offered. Small groups were organized for every two to three rooms with a leader and a hostess. Coffee pots and snacks were brought from home.

A short time after we'd arranged everything as we wanted it, it would be time to tear it down and make the exodus home. Somehow, it never seemed like too much effort in exchange for the activity with special friends. Inconveniences like waiting in line and room mix-ups were minimized by humorous skits inte-

grated into the program of music, testimony, and Bible exposition. Laughter and tears often came from the same face as
women realized the love of God not only proclaimed, but experienced for the first time! Overnighters, like no other gathering,
provide the time needed to bring about these experiences.

Each year the retreat has multiplied, peaking in 1981 with
more than fourteen hundred women in attendance. Even after se-
curing a larger meeting facility, several hundred women had to be
housed in nearby motels. The two ballrooms were able to simul-
taneously accommodate the evening banquet and program; however, this was quite a feat for the musicians and speakers as they
flip-flopped their presentations.

Every year, the committee has watched as each new
Breakaway takes on a personality of its own. When the numbers
peaked at one facility, a mid-week retreat was added. Even with
identical programs, the retreats were each unique. The formats
remain much the same, but the platform messages are always
fresh and timely. Only God can orchestrate messages coming
from very different messengers! Topics have never been assigned,
yet Jill Briscoe's teachings have blended with and complemented
musical testimony by friends like Myrna White, a suburban wife
and mother, and exhortations by guests such as Dr. Helen
Roseveare, a medical missionary who served during the Congo
rebellion. We have watched as the Lord has taken prayers, minds,
and hands and turned our efforts into a sanctuary to proclaim
biblical truths leading to changed hearts and lives.

The evaluations have always revealed many first time decisions
to trust Christ while others report renewed faith—as Jill puts it—
"to keep on keeping on." The committee celebrates, realizing
that these are the rewards of our labors. Of course, we receive a
few discouraging comments too, but, interestingly, the bulk of
the complaints focus on food! We use complaints and suggestions
to make improvements for the next retreat.

We received many requests for a two-night retreat. Offering a
two-night stay gave the women more options, and it became an
overwhelming success. The committee wanted to be flexible,
thinking, "As women's lives and schedules change, let's be ac-
commodating. Women attending can benefit through participating in what they can afford in time and finances." Our theory is
to give them as much of a smorgasbord as we possibly can,

We have watched as the Lord has taken prayers, minds, and hands and turned our efforts into a sanctuary to proclaim biblical truths leading to changed hearts and lives.

allowing them to select and fill their own plates. We've learned that God will work in and through their lives according to their personal response and our interceding prayers.

How does one "do" a Breakaway? With lots of prayer and preparation. Your church may have the ability to host one alone, or you may choose to form an interdenominational network within your Christian community and pool resources to effectively reach women for Christ. It's important to start with some common understandings.

Our Philosophy for Outreach

1. Our approach to ministry is inclusive. That means *whosoever will* is to be invited and accepted on our team and that opportunities for involvement are a high priority (cf. John 3:16).
2. However, *what* is taught and *who* teaches the Word of God is highly guarded. All other areas are subject to risk. Allowances for the freedom to fail and an attitude of "failure is not final" provide an atmosphere in which women are encouraged to experiment in exercising their gifts, thus providing for growth (cf. 2 Timothy 2:15).
3. Our motivation for service arises from gratitude for Christ's work on the cross, not personal recognition (cf. 2 Corinthians 5:14–15; Ephesians 6:7).
4. Our objectives are in line with the Elmbrook Women's Ministries overall purpose—evangelizing, equipping, and encouraging women.
5. As an outreach, our major focus is on Jesus Christ, the one and only way to God. We do not emphasize denominational differences.

Tips to Get Started

Pray—cover the outreach in prayer

Secure a Facility—with good banquet area, seminar rooms, and enough guest rooms.

Get a contract

Secure a Speaker

Establish Package Prices—based on room rate and food prices, with about $8.00 added to the base price to cover costs

Coin a Sponsoring Name—for banking purposes and preparing promotional literature

Acquire Initial Up-front Money—perhaps having each church involved advance a specific amount to cover initial costs (printing, etc.), to be refunded if expenses are met

Begin Basic Planning—
 Develop a theme (have a brainstorming session)
 Develop a coordinating color theme
 Contact a printer available to do brochure
 Contact a graphic artist for brochure, program layout/ design
 Plan the brochure
 Get initial ideas for features

Follow the Monthly Checklist (below)

At your first meeting you will want to establish committee positions and detail responsibilities. Here is a suggested list.

COMMITTEE JOB DESCRIPTIONS

Pulling together a Breakaway weekend can be an exciting and challenging task. The rest of this chapter is dedicated to providing you with concrete ideas and tools for making your Breakaway a successful retreat that will draw women closer to God. Remember that beyond all the details, the goal is to minister to women and to bring each one a step closer in her walk with God. He is faithful, and he will be with you!

Co-Coordinators

Six Months Prior:
 ✓ First committee meeting—brainstorm for theme, seminars, etc.
 ✓ Set dates for monthly meetings
 ✓ Contact main speaker and musicians regarding the chosen theme

Five Months Prior:
 ✓ Contact hotel to verify package prices (needed for early brochure)
 ✓ Distribute list of committee members' phone numbers and addresses
 ✓ Set completion dates for brochure, mail-outs, program

✓ Confirm the seminars as much as possible
✓ Gather list of small-group leaders
✓ Ask committee to keep a diary of frustrations, suggestions, and responsibilities
✓ Inform committee of perks in registration fees offered to committee members
✓ Determine a mailing list; computerize if possible

Four Months Prior:
✓ Check on:
  – Sound
  – Video
  – Bookstore
  – Church publicity procedures
  – Any publications to be offered
✓ Select person to handle scholarships if any are being offered
✓ Arrange promotional skits for use at various churches involved
✓ Design buttons for committee members
✓ Make arrangements for brochures to be handed out at church on Sunday
✓ Reserve dates for registrations to be taken at various churches, if desired

Three Months Prior:
✓ Distribute brochures:
  – Sunday services at various churches
  – Various women's organizations
  – Parachurch groups
  – Bulletin insert at various involved churches
  – Mail out fliers
  – Recruit small-group leaders/hostesses
✓ Distribute scholarship forms to:
  – Small-group leader/chairman
  – Scholarship chairman
  – Both coordinators
✓ Promotion person:
  – Reserve space in bulletin
  – Place announcements in church bulletins as often as possible
  – Announce need for donations for scholarships
  – Order any literature to be distributed

Two Months Prior:
- ✓ Oversee printed program
- ✓ Go to hotel to check large group and seminar ("break-out") rooms
- ✓ Check to see that platform guests have received confirmation letter and a brochure
- ✓ Check all steering committee progress
- ✓ Complete decisions on room arrangements. Meet with hotel personnel with list of needs and requirements (e.g., room setups)
- ✓ Present skits at various church groups
- ✓ Assign shepherds for guest speakers, musicians

One Month Prior:
- ✓ Approve all printing before and after typesetting for:
    - Programs
    - Event sheets (if used)
    - Song sheets (including copyright permission)
    - Evaluation sheets
    - Name tags
- ✓ Check insurance on sound equipment
- ✓ Turn in room arrangements and final room setups to hotel
- ✓ Give information to person making signs and committee/guest name tags
- ✓ Order thank-you gifts (e.g., fruit baskets) for steering committee members, seminar leaders, speakers, and musicians

Month of Retreat:
- ✓ Organize reception for committee, guest speaker, musicians
- ✓ Set next year's Breakaway dates; secure facility and speaker as soon as possible
- ✓ Set up New Christian or follow-up Bible studies
- ✓ Set an evaluation meeting
- ✓ Praise the Lord!

Counseling

Purpose: To provide spiritual, psychological, social, and relational help for the counselee.

The people involved in this area must be trained in counseling services and have available to them an approved list of referrals.

A counseling area is set up at the event, and the trained counselors are available at publicized times. Room setup is usually small tables with two chairs at each, or chairs in groups of two if tables aren't available. Beverages can be provided in this area.

A counseling hostess is usually at the door to greet and encourage women and to place them with a counselor.

Label room with "SHARING and COUNSELING" sign, as it is less theatening than the word "counseling" alone.

Platform

Platform chairperson works with *all* of the events from the main stage. She will work closely with coordinators and the main speaker and will be in charge of:

1. Platform time schedule
2. Special music/accompanists (be aware of copyright laws)
3. Group singing
4. Mixers
5. Choosing (with coordinator) the M.C.
6. Overseeing a committee to decorate stage
7. Determining acts and presentations for platform

Two Months Before:
  ✓ With Breakaway theme in mind, choose songs for group singing. Check copyright laws before reproducing songs
  ✓ Turn in songs to be printed in program
  ✓ Give list of songs to pianist

One Month Before:
  ✓ Line up dinner music, if desired
  ✓ Send microphone set ups to coordinator
  ✓ Determine platform timing with coordinators and main speaker

Prayer

The prayer coordinator gives support and encouragement through prayer to all Breakaway-related events, to all committee members, speakers, and seminar leaders, and to all attending the Breakaway.

Responsibilities

A. Raising prayer support
1. Area churches
2. Women's ministries/parachurch groups
3. Pre-Breakaway prayer breakfast
4. Prepare prayer newsletter, prayer clock, or prayer calendar
B. Conducting prayer breakfast at church for committee members and all interested parties as final preparation for Breakaway
C. Set up and maintain prayer room at Breakaway, open daily throughout event
1. Provide prayer hostesses/volunteers from prayer chain
2. Provide table with prayer helps, tracts, inspirational literature, and sheets for prayer requests
3. Provide room setup: three or four tables, seating six each
D. Conduct early morning (7:00 AM) prayer meetings in prayer room at Breakaway for all who want to attend

Printing and Graphics

The responsibilities of the printing coordinator include the following:

1. Gathering the information to be included in the brochure and program.
2. Tying the information into the theme.
3. Readying the information for printing.
4. Making sure that production deadlines are met.
5. Making sure that the programs arrive at the retreat!
6. Making room signs, name tags, posters.

In the early stages of planning, a theme (including logo, colors, and slogan or verse) should be chosen. This will open up all kinds of opportunity for brainstorming and creative input by the Breakaway committee. They choose the theme that the printing coordinator expands upon and works with.

A production schedule drawn up by the retreat coordinators is presented to each member of the committee. Also, at this time, the person working on the brochure and program should be given the number of finished programs and brochures needed so that paper can be ordered. When ordering paper, it is most cost effective to order for both pieces of material. You will need to know the number of pages in your finished program. Order extra paper so that the printer will have room for error.

Production Schedule

Brochure

- ✓ Six weeks prior to distribution: deadline for all information to be given to printing coordinator.
- ✓ Six to three weeks prior: typeset, proof, pasteup
- ✓ Three to one week prior: printing
- ✓ Three months prior to Breakaway: mailing and distribution

Heads of various committees are responsible for getting information to the printing/graphics coordinator. For instance, the registration committee designs the registration form and gives it to the printing/graphics coordinator.

Typesetting is the process by which a type of print is chosen and all copy is put into that type and size of print for the brochure. Our church does this. The printing coordinator must help choose the type and size and then must proofread the typesetter's work *carefully*. Have the retreat coordinators proofread this also.

Pasteup is the process by which the material (copy, photos, and graphics) is prepared for the printer. The brochure is one piece of paper that is folded. Completely unfold it and you will see that printing is on two sides of one sheet of paper. Two plates are made by the printer—one for each side. Each side must be camera-ready in order to make the plates. A light board, manicure scissors, razor blades, and rubber cement are used to make the copy and photos camera ready. Arrange the copy, photos, and graphics on a light board made especially for this purpose.

Someone with expertise in layout and graphic design is best suited for this job, but God will use anyone with a willing heart!

Printed Program

- ✓ Seven weeks prior to Breakaway: Deadline for all information to be given to printing coordinator
- ✓ Seven to five weeks prior: Typeset, proof, pasteup
- ✓ Five to three weeks prior: Print program
- ✓ Two weeks prior: Collate and staple (We hired the printer to do this.)

The printing/graphics coordinator must work closely with the retreat coordinators so that all necessary information is included in both pieces of material.

It should be established very early on what people are responsible for getting certain information to the printing coordinator. For instance, in regard to the program, the seminar descriptions should be provided by the team responsible for the seminars.

Coordinating all of this information with the theme chosen by the retreat committee will be the responsibility of the printing coordinator. This can be lots of fun. For the 1989 retreat we began thinking of as many phrases and words common to the theme of a cruise as we could. This included song titles and nautical and ship lingo. This list got us going and into the necessary thinking mode.

Note: Your program and brochure need not only to be interesting and appealing, but also clear and concise. Don't sacrifice being clear for being clever!

Having two people work on this stage is helpful. A good, healthy brainstorming session can get you started.

Once you have the copy ready, it needs to be clearly written out for the typesetter. We now do this on a computer. It makes her job much easier to have the copy typed page for page.

Copy will include a schedule, seminar descriptions, biographical materials for seminar leaders and main speakers. Anything *written* is copy. Pages to be presented to the printer must be camera-ready.

The first year one does the job of printing coordinator, a lot of learning takes place. By the second year, the process is clearer and the job much easier. For this reason, we recommend that an

Don't sacrifice being clear for being clever!

assistant be used the second year so that another person can learn the job and be the responsible person the following year with a new assistant. This gives many women the opportunity to learn a new skill and provides an experienced printing coordinator each year.

The responsibility can seem overwhelming, but nothing is more fun than seeing the finished project and knowing you did your best for *God's* glory. He will be glorified if you obey him and do what you can to make the retreat a success. Don't worry about being trained for the job. Just do your best, ask for help, and have others proofread the copy!

Publicity

The responsibility of the publicity coordinator is to publicize the event within the churches involved as well as to the general public. Target areas include your immediate area, your state, and any contiguous states. The means for doing this is open for creativity and resourcefulness.

A. General guidelines
 1. Work through the appropriate church channels
 2. Use Breakaway or church letterhead for all press releases and public service announcements
 3. Know and meet various deadlines

B. Publicity possibilities
 1. Area churches
   a. Bulletin announcements
   b. Bulletin insert
   c. Information desk registrations
   d. Promotion Sunday—lobby
   e. Gift certificates
   f. Scholarships
 2. Women's Ministries studies
   a. Mailing
   b. Newsletter announcements
   c. Brochure distributions
   d. Skits
   e. Invitations
   f. Flyers
 3. General public
   a. Area Christian bookstores

    b. Christian newspapers or newsletters

    c. News releases to area newspapers

    d. Public service announcement to area radio and TV stations

    e. Flyers and brochures to area churches

Strategy and Calendar

Nine-to-Six Months Prior:

✓ Announce dates and featured speakers in any church mailings

Three Months Prior:

✓ Mail brochures

✓ Present promotional skits at various churches

✓ Advertise gift certificate availability at various churches

Two Months Prior:

✓ Advertise in local Christian newspaper

✓ Send news releases and public service announcements to available radio stations and newspapers *three weeks* before the registration deadline

✓ Repeat skits at various churches, with brochure distribution

✓ Continue gift-certificate announcements

✓ Distribute posters to churches, local business places, public bulletin boards

Remember that one-to-one publicity is the best publicity!

Remember that one-to-one publicity is the best publicity.

Registration

Registration for Breakaway involves four separate parts:

1. Working with the coordinator(s) and printing coordinator to put together the registration form for the brochure.

2. Processing the registrations. This involved putting registrants into rooms, alphabetizing the registrations, making name tags, keeping track of money and making sure it matches the requested registration, and keeping a running total of registrations and special requests for rooming.

3. Working with the hotel in setting up rooms. Let them know any special needs or requests; make sure enough rooms are set apart for the event. You may want to secure

a special block of rooms for the Breakaway committee, keynote speaker, and other V.I.P.'s. Arrange for early registration/check-in for guests, committee.

4. Running registration the day of the event. This involves recruiting enough workers, dividing the registration into alphabetical breakdowns, working with the hotel to assign specific rooms, giving out name tags, and setting up a special table for questions and problems.

Now we computerize the registrations, making it much easier to keep track of registration, print name tags, and make lists of registrants for the hotel by room.

Seminars

Contact potential seminar leaders, confirm definite commitments to lead seminars, and do all planning necessary for the successful presentation of each seminar.

The number and types of seminars and presentation times depends on your projected attendance, the type of audience, and the theme of the conference. (Plan about six to eight offerings for four-to-five hundred attendees, plus a sing-along and aerobics.)

A. Choosing Seminars

Seminars are determined at a steering committee meeting after the main conference theme has been designated. Ideas will pop up as you "brainstorm" the general theme. Some ideas to consider:

Prayer

How to study the Bible

Spiritual gifts

Forgiveness

Marriage

Stress

Codependency

Parenting

Caring for aged parents

Financial planning

Decoration tips

Basket making

Sweatshirt painting

Stenciling
Bow making

A book study or a film (e.g., World Wide Pictures) is an option. In addition to the regular seminars these are always good:

Late-night and early morning aerobics
Water aerobics
A late-night sing-along

Choose a balance of spiritual, need-oriented, and fun seminars. Tie the seminar titles in with the general theme (e.g., a marriage seminar might be entitled *Marriage* on *the Rock*.)

B. Choose Seminar Speakers
   1. Presenters are discussed and recommended at the Steering Committee meeting.
   2. Contact by phone or letter for the initial request. State dates, times, topic, and policy.
      a. Our church members are expected to do seminars at no fee. We do, however, cover the cost of Breakaway.
      b. Out-of-church feature speakers are given the cost of the Breakaway, mileage or transportation, and an honorarium.
      c. Speakers must be cleared with the Women's Pastor before contact.
      d. All speakers are required to sign a statement of faith so we do not have any basic conflicts in material presented.
   3. Approximately two to three months before Breakaway, send a letter confirming dates, topics, times, registration procedure, and a request for information for the printed program. *Set a deadline for return.*
   4. Send another confirmation letter about three weeks later, requesting any book titles that might be recommended and the policy for handouts.
   5. Contact by phone any who do not reply!

C. Room Setups
   Meet with coordinators and hotel staff if necessary to assign seminars to rooms. Give speakers' setups to

coordinators for turning in to hotel (microphones, chair arrangement, podium, flip charts). *Always* ask for ice and water in each presenter's room.

D. Printed Program

Complete the seminar information received from speakers. Edit, correct, and give to printing coordinator by the deadline, along with the *times of presentation* and the rooms that will be used.

E. Follow up on Seminar Speakers' Registrations

Give a list of speakers to registration chairperson. If registrations do not come in, contact the speakers about this.

F. Programs

If programs are completed well in advance, send one to each speaker along with room assignment for presentation and information on handouts.

G. Hostess

Assign a Hostess to each seminar time to help out in any way.

H. Signs

Make a list of signs that will be needed to mark the seminar rooms, and turn it in to the person in charge of printing.

I. On the day of Breakaway:
   1. Bring handouts and signs (or know where these are!)
   2. Put up signs at seminar rooms. Check with hotel about how they want the signs attached.
   3. Check each seminar room for correct setup.
   4. Keep an attendance count for each presentation.

J. After the Breakaway

Send a thank you to each seminar leader and hostess.

Small-Group Leaders

Being a small-group leader at Breakaway can be the highlight of your Breakaway experience. Small-group leaders are women who are recommended by leaders in the church on the basis of their Christian walk, church involvement, and desire to serve God in this capacity. In our church, these women are approved by a committee of leaders of the Women's Ministries.

Six weeks prior to Breakaway, there is a training session for the leaders. It is usually held on a Saturday morning at the church building. A letter is sent to each woman inviting her to be a leader and asking her to attend the meeting. She is asked to select someone to be her hostess. Usually it is a close friend or relative. The hostess should also attend the training session.

At the training session, the women learn about what is happening at Breakaway. They are given an autobiography of the featured speaker, any worksheets that the speaker will be using, and the small-group activities. Jill is there to go over her outline for the Bible study. We go over the schedule for Breakaway and explain the layout of the hotel. They are given basic instructions on leading small groups, and there is time for questions.

There are two small-group activities that are held in the leaders' rooms. The prelude group meets Friday night before the banquet. This is a fun time of getting to know the women in your group. An icebreaker is played to help the women get to know each other. The prelude group usually lasts about forty-five minutes. The second time the groups meet is after Jill's Bible study on Saturday morning. This is a very special time of sharing and discussing Jill's talk. Many decisions for Christ are made at this time. The small-group session lasts about thirty minutes.

Small-group leaders play an important role during Breakaway. For many of the women attending Breakaway, the small-group times are the most rewarding aspect of their Breakaway experience.

SUGGESTED BREAKAWAY POLICIES

No children will be permitted to attend.

Registrants will be housed together only when registrations are mailed together in the same envelope.

Registration preferences will be honored by postal date.

Set registration deadlines, late fees, and refund policies.

A waiting list will be used to fill up last-minute cancellations.

SUGGESTIONS FOR SMALL-GROUP LEADERS

I. You are a servant: Serve.

Pray.

Create an environment of warmth. Seek to make the people you are leading feel at home.

Be flexible. Try not to have specific expectations about the people you will be leading, or how everything will go. Be expectant, but give room to move, even in your expectations.

Accept the fact that you will like some people better than others. That's O.K. Your responsibility is to love them all, in the sense of wanting God's best for them and giving them all your best. You are a servant.

Never apologize or comment that this is your first time as a leader or that you are afraid. Do not call unnecessary attention to yourself.

Never compare the group you are working with or the situation in which you are ministering to any other group or situation.

Be sensitive to women's needs. Do not take a group past the scheduled time.

Be under proper authority. If materials or methods have been prescribed, use them.

II. You are a leader: Lead.

Pray.

You are responsible, under God, for what takes place in the situation you are leading. You have been prayerfully chosen, and we are assuming you have prayed over your own position as a leader. Now lead.

You are responsible for not allowing control of the situation to pass to a person in the group. If someone begins to dominate or to direct the group into an undesirable channel, you must bring them back.

You must be thoroughly prepared both by study and prayer. Then you must trust God. It is not a forceful personality or a strident voice that is needed, but the power of God, through you, his faithful under-shepherd.

III. You are a person: Be yourself.

Pray.

Choose the clothes you will wear well in advance of the time you will be leading. See that they are clean, put them in a special place in your closet, and then forget them.

Use your own vocabulary and illustrations. Illustrations make the rounds and get very shopworn. Ask God to give you your own fresh ones, from your own life.

Think about your own style: are you casual, formal, reserved, outgoing? Ask God to help you use, not deny your own personality type, to bring it into play and into balance.

Forget yourself.

A WORD TO THE WISE

Breakaway can be a marvelous experience for many. However, it isn't unusual for women to feel their loneliest when in a crowd of women who seem "all together" and seem to have a heap of friends. People are more important than programs and we try to instill this philosophy in the hearts of every Breakaway helper. The core purpose for the hospitality ministry is to reach out to hurting or lonely women. We must do our best to ensure fewer and fewer women slip through the cracks at our programs and special events, but it is a tough job. Only with the Holy Spirit's whispered inclinations can we bind those broken hearts out there. The following article has been used by permission as a warning and an incentive to make our outreaches all that God would want them to be.

Perspective

Ask No Quarter

It wasn't unusual for Mildred (not her real name) to carry a couple of rolls of quarters in her purse; she was assistant treasurer at her church.

Mildred was in her early 60s, devout, sweet, and still in pain over the death of her husband six months before. Her divorced twenty-five-year-old son of indeterminate sexual and pharmaceutical preference had recently moved back home. That added stress was not good for Mildred's bad back, arthritis, and allergies.

She had long since given up trying to talk to her friends or her pastor about her troubles. They seemed to avoid her. She was one lonely woman, with all her emotional and spiritual needs in one basket: her first-ever women's retreat. What a beautiful word. *Retreat*. She needed this retreat at any cost.

She began the three-hundred-mile drive on a blistering Monday morning with high hopes of refreshment, of spiritual renewal, of finding new friends, maybe someone she could open up to, someone who would listen, care, love her.

Over a dollar and a half lunch, Mildred gazed at the brochure, rehearsing the many credits of the speaker. Beautiful, talented, widely published, a pastor's wife. How wonderful to have it all together.

When she arrived at the conference center at three that afternoon, she was soaked with perspiration. Shy in a new setting, she lugged her belongings to the registration desk. The rooms wouldn't be ready for a couple of hours, and dinner was three hours hence.

Then, the break of a lifetime! One of the retreat directors was looking for someone with a car to who was willing to pick up the speaker at the airport. Would she? Would she ever!

Exhausted, intimidated, yet thrilled, Mildred located the speaker and helped carry her bags to the car. "And what is your role with the retreat, dear?"

"Just an attendee. They needed someone to pick you up."

"Oh. Be careful with the bag, hon. It's leather."

Mildred loaded the trunk. On the way back, the conversation centered on the speaker, her husband, her books, her schedule, her home, her children. Mildred broached the subject of her own son. "Sounds like an ingrate," the speaker said. "I don't know if I could handle that. Do you know when dinner is?"

The setting sun brought little break in the temperature. Everyone sat fanning themselves, waiting for dinner, still two hours off. As soon as she could, the speaker extricated herself from the humble chauffeur and became the center of attention. Mildred tried to join the conversation, but was ignored.

She felt plain and simple, unimportant and lonely. Until someone discovered the pop machine. Those who had quarters had enough for only one can each. The registration cash box had been put away. Sticky, miserable, suffocating women offered each other dollar bills for two quarters.

Demand quickly outran supply. Before long, two hundred women were in desperate need of change. When it seemed all had resigned themselves to frustration, Mildred slowly rose and moved toward the machine, fishing a roll of quarters from her purse and deftly breaking it open. The coins' clanking and the can's thumping brought a crowd.

Mildred happily made change and accepted the smiles and thanks, drinking in the attention that was every bit as refreshing as the pop. And there stood the speaker. The superstar. In need.

"Uh, Minnie, was it?"

"Mildred."

"Yes, Mildred. Tell me again the name of that daughter I promised to pray for."

"It was my son."

"Oh, yes. And your church. You're active there, you said?"
Mildred nodded.

"And Mildred, did you have any more change?"

—Jerry B. Jenkins
from *Moody Monthly*, October 1987

Chapter 13

Reaching Out Through Special Events

Special events are often highlights in the ministry year. They draw people who might not otherwise participate in church-associated activities and provide an opportunity for women to get involved and serve in many different areas. When planning a special event, it is important to define the purpose or goal in advance. The purpose and group you wish to target will determine the type of event you plan. Here are a few examples:

Purpose	*Target Audience*	*Type of Event*
Fellowship and Fun	Women	Brunch
Evangelism	Women	Victorian Tea
	Children	Birthday Party for Jesus
	Executives	Executives' Dinner
Personal Growth/	Women	Leadership Retreat
Renewal	Women	Breakaway
Family Fun/	Families	Carnival
Fundraising		

In most of this chapter we'll share step-by-step instructions for putting on seven different evangelistic events that have been effective outreach tools for us at Elmbrook. Four are designed for reaching women (a brunch, English tea, Christmas coffee, and craft ministry); one is intended for children (a Birthday Party for Jesus); one is planned for entire families (a Wild, Wild West Family Fun Day); and one is implemented to enrich all ministries (Evangelism Training across the Ministries). We hope many of you will become excited about the possibilities for reaching out to non-Christians through special events like these.

Before we discuss the "how-tos" for particular events, let's talk about some of the initial details, all of which should be decided about six months before the event. The birth of a special event begins with a brainstorming session. Assemble your creative team and event coordinator(s) together to brainstorm ideas and themes. Choose a theme that will allow many possibilities for speaker, programming, music, special features, and decorations.

Determine the date, time, location, and possible cost of the event. Consider competing church and school events as well as family vacation times or holidays. A well-timed event is apt to be more successful. Many events will be held at church, but others may attract more people if they are held at other facilities. The cost of an event may be covered by ticket sales, a registration fee, or a love-gift offering taken at the event itself.

When you have the date and time decided, contact desired speakers and musicians for availability. Confirming your featured speakers and entertainers should be done as soon as possible to avoid problems in further details of planning and implementation.

Establish a committee of interested and available people to plan and carry out all the details of the event. Most of our events have required similar committee positions, and each position has defined responsibilities.

Coordinator(s)—Responsible for planning and overseeing all the details of the event. Schedules and leads meetings. Communicates with committee heads as needed. Evaluates the event when completed.

Secretary—Responsible for recording information covered at meetings. Schedules and reserves rooms for meetings and childcare. Reminds committee of meeting dates.

Prayer—Responsible for committing the event to prayer at every meeting.

Promotion/Publicity—Responsible for design and production of flyers, posters, invitations, and tickets as needed. Schedules promotion for local media, church bulletins, church newsletters, and for various women's groups throughout the church. Promotion may take the form of skits and announcements.

Ticket Sales/Registration—Reserves space and schedules dates for ticket sales or registration. Schedules workers and communicates number of registrants to the necessary committee members (e.g., nursery, food). Is accountable for handling money and transferring it to the treasurer.

Decorations—Responsible for designing and submitting room setup. Coordinates decorations with the chosen theme of the event. Purchases supplies for appropriate decorations. Organizes workers to help with room setup and creation of decorations and special giveaway favors.

Program—Responsible for planning program for the event. Initiates contact with and confirms speaker, musicians, and any special features. Submits stage and sound needs to decorations for master setup plan. Content of presentation must be approved by coordinator(s). Provides all program participants with agenda for the event.

Kitchen—Determines menu and kitchen requirements. Schedules staff for preparation, serving, and cleanup. Responsible for purchasing food if necessary.

Nursery—Determines child capacity for each area. Responsible for adequate staffing in each area. Must update nursery needs as registration indicates. Closes nursery registration when at capacity.

Treasurer—Determines budget for the event. Reimburses receipts submitted. Responsible for money collected at registration or love-gift offering at the event. Provides accounting of all transactions following the event.

A WOMEN'S BRUNCH

Women's ministry has the tradition of serving a brunch to kick off the fall schedule and to conclude in the spring. The kickoff brunch provides an opportunity for fellowship and is generally more evangelistic in nature. Women may invite unchurched friends to hear the gospel message and learn more about the women's programs being offered. The setting is one of warmth and fellowship. The spring brunch provides a time for fellowship and reflection on the past year.

Following is a step-by-step guide for planning a successful brunch.

Preparing for the Brunch

Three Months Prior:
✓ Meet with committee heads to finalize theme, program, decorations, and menu
✓ Design and produce attractive invitation, which should include program, contact person, and tear-off registration

Two Months Prior:
✓ Confirm speaker, musicians, and any special features
✓ Print invitations and/or tickets
✓ Distribute invitations at church or through the mail
✓ Encourage women to invite friends if brunch is evangelistic

Six Weeks Prior:
✓ Begin promotion and publicity at church
- Bulletin board
- Article in the church newsletter
- Announcements and skits at women's groups
- More invitations

One Month Prior:
✓ Promote event in church bulletin
✓ Reserve space at church for registration personnel
✓ Prepare sign-up sheets for food donations, setup, cleanup, and kitchen help
✓ Committee meets to finalize details in all areas

Three Weeks Prior:
✓ Registration and/or ticket sales begin
✓ Repeat bulletin announcement and promote at church groups
✓ Final purchase of decoration and giveaway items
✓ Registration updates nursery and food committees with attendance count

Two Weeks Prior:
✓ Continue registration, and repeat bulletin announcement

✓ Decoration committee completes setup plan for brunch

✓ Program committee adds stage and sound needs to establish order

✓ Registration updates nursery and food with new numbers

✓ All money is now turned over to the treasurer

One Week Prior:

✓ Determine final count and give to food, nursery, and decoration committees

✓ Submit final facility setup sheet

✓ Complete decorations and giveaway items

✓ Purchase last-minute food items that are not donated

✓ Meet with committee heads if needed to finalize details

✓ Generate program agenda for all participants

✓ Schedule kitchen, setup, and cleanup help

✓ Set up and decorate the day or evening before the brunch

Two Weeks After:

✓ Coordinator(s) meet with committee heads to evaluate the brunch

"Pearls of Wisdom"

One year the theme for the brunch, "Pearls of Wisdom," was drawn from Women's Ministries' overall theme of "The Way of Wisdom." The decorations were designed around the brunch theme. Tables were set with white doily place mats and lavender napkins. Violets were wrapped with flowered ribbon and pearls. They were placed on a round mirror with two votive candles. Three long tables on either side of the room served as buffet tables. Single long tables in each corner of the room contained beverages. The stage backdrop was a white lattice work with lavender ribbon, flowers, and greenery. The giveaways at each place were small nosegays (violets and baby's breath wrapped with a small doily and tied with lavender ribbon and pearls).

REACHING OUT THROUGH AN EVANGELISTIC HIGH TEA

Picture yourself seated at a table draped with a soft lace cloth, adorned with delicate garden-fresh blossoms in assorted teapots, all bathed in the golden glow of candlelight. Delicious finger sandwiches and pastries overflow from delicate silver trays, while the fragrance of freshly cut flowers and the aroma of hot English tea delight the senses. A beautiful Victorian Tea with all the trimmings has been set for you and a guest. Sound inviting? With a little creativity and a meshing of the old, the new, and the borrowed, you can host a high tea that will not only touch women's senses, but their hearts for Jesus as well.

> **With a little creativity and a meshing of the old, the new, and the borrowed, you can host a high tea that will not only touch women's senses, but also their hearts for Jesus as well.**

Selecting a Theme

After you have selected a committee and ironed out the initial details outlined at the beginning of this chapter, you must focus on your theme. One of the exciting things about planning a high tea is that there are a myriad of possibilities for the kind you'll feature. You could have a "Victorian Mad Hatter" tea where everyone comes adorned in a beautiful vintage hat, for example. You may want to feature a less formal tea, or you could have a "Royal High Tea" like ours. Brainstorm together, have fun with it, and make it your own.

Once you decide on what type of tea you'll have, selecting the theme will be easy. Our speaker helped us out in this decision. She chose the title of her talk, "Royalty, Roses, and a Cup of Tea," based on our plans. We then used that title for our theme and all of our publicity for the event.

Selecting the Location

> **Will this be an attractive, comfortable, and nonthreatening setting for your unchurched friend?**

Next, you'll want to think through carefully where you will host your tea. There are a wide variety of places that will work nicely for this type of an event, including your church fellowship hall. This option would certainly be the least expensive if cost is a big factor for your event. If not, you might consider featuring the tea at a local Women's Club, country club, or hotel. Because the event is designed for the non-Christian (remember, it's evangelistic!) ask yourself, will this be an attractive, comfortable, and nonthreatening setting for your unchurched friend? These concerns are important when deciding your location and should be dedicated to prayer. Again, if you're working with a tight budget, your location choice may already be determined.

Selecting the Menu

Because our women desired to make and serve our own food, we decided on our church location for the event. We transformed our fellowship hall into a spectacular Victorian Garden graced with cascading flowers and bathed in soft, glowing candlelight. After careful research, the food committee created an English menu featuring scrumptious cucumber, cala lilly, and ribbon sandwiches, scones, seasonal fruit, raspberry diamonds, meringues with lemon, chocolate truffles, and of course, hot English tea garnished with fresh lemon.

Selecting the Invitations

The invitations and promotion were the next areas to be addressed. We kept the design of the invitations very simple, yet elegant, using a Mac computer with border designs. In addition to the printed invitations that were created and distributed, flyers were made and given to all of our women's Bible studies for reinforced advertising. Our promotional materials included the restriction that women could not attend the event unless they brought a non-Christian friend.

Women were reminded throughout our advertising of the purpose for the event. We emphasized that this was not an event designed for you to bring your closest Christian friends, but rather an opportunity to be used for evangelism.

Enclosed was a reply card with a place for the woman's name, telephone number, and name of guest(s). It also included the $7.00 per person cost of the event along with the deadline for the reply. At the very bottom of the reply card we printed "Space is limited, so please make your reservations early!"

Selecting Hostesses

The tables, which sat eight women each, quickly filled. For each table we appointed a table hostess who was responsible for welcoming the women at her table and making sure their tea cups always remained full. She was also responsible for the actual decorating of her table in the victorian/royalty theme. Each hostess brought her own fine china and silver from home along with an assorted flower arrangement flowing from a unique teapot or china piece. This individual table decor helped with the overall decoration of the hall. All of the flowers for the table were pur-

We emphasized that this was not an event designed for you to bring your closest Christian friends, but rather an opportunity to be used for evangelism.

chased at one local flower shop for consistency. Each hostess covered the $15.00–$20.00 cost of the flowers for her table as part of her agreement for hostessing; however, the women's ministry made up the difference for those who couldn't afford it.

Selecting the Program

Now comes the fun part—planning the actual program. We knew our Victorian Garden wouldn't be complete without the soft sounds of music, so we hired a harpist who filled the hall with music as our guests arrived. Upon arrival, guests were seated (place cards with each woman's name were preprinted and placed on the tables beforehand). A table chart at the registration table helped make seating easy.

Our mistress of ceremonies welcomed the women and posed the question, "If you could have tea with anyone, who would it be, and why?" This question was discussed at the tables while delicious delicacies were served. Within minutes the room filled with the hum of friendly chatter.

A guest artist performed a classical rendition of "Jesus Loves Me" followed by our speaker who gave an evangelistic message interweaving the ideas, "Royalty, Roses, and a Cup of Tea." The afternoon was simply delightful!

In closing, follow-up cards had been placed at each table. Those women requesting additional information were sent packets containing the booklet *Becoming a Christian* by John Stott, as well as other follow-up materials. Several weeks later they were contacted and asked if they had any questions about Christianity or ministry opportunities.

With a little ingenuity, creativity, and hard work, your women can feature an Evangelistic High Tea that is sure to be remembered long after it's over. It will likely become a treasured tradition that women will eagerly look forward to bringing their seeking friends to year after year.

Just think—one magical afternoon of days-gone-by might just change a woman's heart for eternity!

SHARING CHRIST AT A CHRISTMAS COFFEE

Christmas offers strategic opportunities for reaching your community with the love of Christ. One way to reach women (or couples) with the gospel is through hosting special Christmas

> **Just think—one magical afternoon of days-gone-by might just change a woman's heart for eternity!**

Coffees during the holidays. A holiday home is an ideal environment to communicate the true meaning of Christmas. No season lends itself more easily to homespun entertaining and timeless truth. Hosting these coffees takes little effort, but can reap a beautiful harvest, as women are given the opportunity to hear the gospel message in the home of a friend. Two women are usually needed to pull together an evangelistic coffee. One opens her home to her neighbors and friends, serving as hostess, while another serves as the speaker. The following "how to's" will help your women plan and hostess successful coffees in their homes.

Sample Schedule*

9:30 AM–10:00AM	Greetings, coffee and snacks (an icebreaker telling a little about each person can be helpful here)
10:00 AM–10:30 AM	Introductions and message
10:30 AM–11:00 AM	Mingling and any games, gifts, or ornament exchanges (be sure to allow time for guests to talk with you and the speaker)

Note: Coffees can also be held in the evening.

Invitations

Invitations should be sent out two weeks to ten days prior to your coffee. Each invitation should state clearly, "I have invited a friend to share a brief inspirational message on the true meaning of Christmas." This way, your friends won't be surprised when your speaker shares her message. Hand delivering invitations will give you an opportunity to introduce yourself. An RSVP on the invitation will also help you prepare.

Preparation

Preparation begins with prayer, followed by prayer, and more prayer. Friends, family and your church are valuable resources. Pray with your speaker. Share specific concerns.

Meet with your speaker in your home ahead of time. Tell her your plan and listen to her message. This is *your* coffee. Be sure you feel comfortable with your speaker and her message before your coffee.

Child Care

Coffees can be held with children present; however, the message will have fewer distractions if only adults are present. If you have your coffee on a day when child care isn't available, you can:

- Make child care available at a neighbor's house. Ask someone to baby-sit as a ministry.
- Baby-sit for another coffee hostess and have her baby-sit for you.
- Arrange child care in another room of your house.

Hospitality

Use every resource available to extend the warmth and love of Christ. Music icebreakers, hot coffee, good food, decorations, potpourri, and games can all add to the message.

Talks

The messages should be presented by godly women who are mature in their faith and love, and are able to field questions and lead women to a personal commitment to Christ. Messages should be about ten minutes in length and contain a complete gospel message. It should be clear what is necessary for salvation. Personal testimonies, children's books, Christmas carols, and object lessons can all be made into effective talks.

Church Ministry

A training session can be offered to your women's ministry or the church body at large. It is recommended that the training be arranged as an actual Christmas Coffee for speakers and hostesses to experience. Following the presentation of the message, speakers and hostesses can be separated for specific instructions.

A BIRTHDAY PARTY FOR JESUS

Every December, young and old alike celebrate the birth of the baby Jesus at a very special party. Ten years ago several young mothers looked for a meaningful way to present the real message of Christmas to their children. They developed a Birthday Party for Jesus, which has evolved into a celebration enjoyed by hundreds of children and adults each year. The event is planned, staffed, and sponsored by Moms and More Ministry.

The Birthday Party for Jesus also provides women and children a new and exciting evangelistic opportunity. In a season that preoccupies the world with Santa and shopping, we offer an eternal alternative. By inviting other children, relatives, friends, and neighbors, we help others focus on the birth of Christ and its significance. The party has enabled many to share the Gospel message in a pleasant, welcoming setting.

When planning a Birthday Party for Jesus, it is important to establish a purpose and guidelines to follow. Our purpose is to share the good news of Christ's birth with children both in the church and in the community.

Preparing for the Party

Three Months Prior:
✓ Design and produce an attractive invitation (including important information, name of contact person, and tear-off registration form) that will appeal to women both inside and outside the church
✓ Finalize details of program
✓ Meet with committee heads

Six-to-Eight Weeks Prior:
✓ Print invitations/tickets (if applicable)
✓ Meet with committee heads

Four Weeks Prior:
✓ Distribute invitations to area churches, area preschools, church women's groups, community groups
✓ Encourage church women to take extra invitations for inviting others
✓ Begin media coverage and promotion
✓ Send a media packet containing invitations and a short cover letter explaining the event to Christian newspapers, local newspapers, area churches for bulletins, radio and TV stations
✓ Meet with committee heads

Three Weeks Prior:
✓ Begin registration and ticket sales

✓ Check all information on registration form and make sure money is enclosed (we have found that $2.00 per person covers costs)

✓ Send each registrant an envelope with tickets and name tags for pre-labeling children, avoiding a registration table the day of the party

✓ Include toy list and non-perishable food items for donations to needy families

Two Weeks Prior:
✓ Print placemats, programs, craft instructions
✓ Meet with committee heads

One Week Prior:
✓ Determine final count
✓ Finalize setup and room arrangements
✓ Complete shopping for food and crafts
✓ Assemble craft and treat bags
✓ Meet with committee heads for finalization

Remember to pray about your plans every step of the way!

We also set up several guidelines: determine the age-range of the children to be reached and plan an age-appropriate party. A program that is not geared to the age of the children will not be effective. We focused on reaching little hearts (two-to-five-year-olds) for Jesus. Offering diversified activities keeps little ones interested and occupied for fifteen-to-twenty minutes in any one area. Determine the elements to be included: prayer, worship, music, entertainment, crafts, fellowship. Make sure to share the message of Christ's birth and the importance of making a personal decision for Christ. It is important that the message is repeated in different forms throughout the party.

A Sample Birthday Party for Jesus

(Approximately a two-hour program)

Greeters positioned at doors will serve to welcome children and adults and will be important in making visitors feel welcome.

Allow fifteen minutes for nursery check-in and for people to hang coats, pick up a program, and be seated.

Time Allotted	*Program*
5 minutes	Welcome, Announcements, Prayer
10 minutes	Story or drama presentation with message
10 minutes	Sharing gifts—children are invited to place their gifts for needy families beneath a Christmas tree or at the manger. This is an excellent time to talk about sharing and caring.
10–15 minutes	Music and singing
15 minutes	Walk through Bethlehem or a live nativity. Pre-school children learn most by touch, taste, and feel. By walking through a re-creation of Bethlehem, they experience the excitement of Christ's birth firsthand. (This has been the most effective and memorable part of the party for our children.)
15 minutes	Light entertainment with a message. This is another opportunity to reach those you may have missed with the story or drama. Have fun with a clown, ventriloquist, or puppet show, all built around the theme of the program.
15 minutes	Crafts—Everyone is invited to a decorated party room for crafts. Each table is decorated with a centerpiece designed around the party theme. Birthday party "coloring book" placemats and crayons are placed within reach of little fingers. A plastic zip-loc bag contains a take-home coloring project, supplies, and instructions for making an ornament in remembrance of the day.
15 minutes	Treats—As crafts are finished, ice cream dixie cups with candles, cookies, or a cupcake and juice or coffee are passed out. (A breakfast for Jesus may feature cold cereal or donuts, juice and hot chocolate.) The lights are dimmed, the candles are lit, and the children sing "Happy Birthday" to Jesus.

And what party is complete without a treat bag filled with goodies? Raisins, chocolate kisses, M & M's, a "Happy Birthday, Jesus" pencil, and a booklet with the Christmas story are neatly packaged in a white bag tied with a colorful ribbon and a red or green balloon.

This year give a Birthday Party for Jesus and share God's gift of Jesus. There are many wonderful books and helpful resource materials available to you at the library and Christian bookstores.

HOSTING A FAMILY FUN DAY

Another type of event providing fun and fellowship is the Family Fun Day. This idea grew out of a desire to offer a special event designed especially for families. The entire Women's Ministries team combined their time and talents to produce a memorable and effective event. We had three goals in mind when we met to brainstorm this event:

1. The project would offer women in all areas of ministry the opportunity to work together toward a common goal while serving the Lord.
2. The event would provide fun, fellowship, and entertainment for the entire family.
3. Proceeds from the event would help underwrite ministry childcare costs not covered by the church and provide seed money for future events of its kind.

Promoting the project, which we called Wild, Wild, West Family Fun Day, began in the fall. Every woman was encouraged to participate in some way, either individually or as a Bible study group. We used skits, songs, and informational announcements in all of our women's groups. Publicity began one month before the event, with advertising in a local Christian newspaper and the church newsletter. Three weeks before the event, large posters were printed and distributed and the church bulletin board was decorated. An informational flyer was distributed to girls and boys in Pioneer clubs two weeks before the event. One week prior to the event, flyers were distributed to all Sunday school children, fifth grade and under. We gave away nearly a thousand brightly colored helium balloons that day to the children in the lobby of the church. Our pastor also announced the event that

Sunday. This aggressive campaign of promotion and publicity contributed to the overall success of the Family Fun Day.

Three months before the event women were asked to complete a form committing themselves to be responsible for a specific booth or task. The form listed twenty-five game booths, eight food booths, an entertainment stage, and many other areas in which women could be involved.

Ticket sales began two weeks before the event. Women sold them at church and at various women's groups. Tickets sold before the event were priced at five for $1.00, while they were four for $1.00 at the door. Most of the games required one ticket, and the craft booths required two tickets. The number of tickets redeemed for food was determined by the food committee and the treasurer. Tickets also purchased black and white cow balloons and an assortment of cowboy hats; both sold out long before the day was over. The ticket committee determined the quantity of

---

Game Booths

Tootsie Tug, Shoot Out, Duck Pond, Face Painting, Gold Nugget, Dig Spin Art, Fish Pond, Ring Toss, Bean Bag Toss, Treat Walk, Obstacle Course, Clothespin in Bottle, Little Tykes Rocking Horses, Basketball Shoot, Frisbee Through Hula Hoop, Evangelistic Bolo Ties, Evangelistic Bracelets, Tiny Tyke Tunnel of Fun, Nerf Shoot Out, Jail, Cow Chip Hockey, Long Horn Long Jump, Western Polaroid Pics, Little Tykes Wagon Train Ride, Velcro Man.

Food Booths

Hot dogs, Pizza, Nachos and Pretzels with Cheese, Popcorn and Licorice, Cotton Candy, Beverages, Bakery, Ice Cream.

Help Needed

General setup, general cleanup, kitchen crew, table maintenance, bathroom maintenance, greeting and ministry info table, ticket sales, entertainment stage, decorations, prizes, balloon and hat sales.

tickets needed and ordered them from the Oriental Trading catalog one month before the event.

The prize committee was responsible for choosing prizes and determining the quantity needed for the game booths. Since this was a new type of event for us, we called on the expertise of women who had been involved in similar carnivals in area schools. They helped us choose prizes that most children liked. Most prizes were ordered from Oriental Trading about one month before the event. Prizes were supplemented with a variety of candy and treats purchased from a local Sam's Club. Leftover, unopened candy was returnable and an area school purchased the remaining prizes for their own carnival.

General setup consisted of rolling a large protective tarp over the gym floor, placing tables and chairs in each of the booth areas, carrying bales of hay to each booth, and arranging props and decorations. The cleanup crew cleared everything off the tarp, swept it clean, and rolled it back up after the event.

Women helping with general decorations came to several work days. They designed and painted western scenery and props placed throughout the gym and fellowship hall on the day of the event. The work days proved to be great fun for all who participated.

The food booths were situated in the Fellowship Hall near the kitchen. Women choosing these booths were asked to set up, staff, and clean up their area. The food committee was responsible for determining the types of food to sell and the quantities to order. Final orders were placed a week to ten days before the event. A local food distributor allowed us to return any unused and unopened items. This helped us avoid purchasing more than was necessary. Tombstone Pizza gave us a freezer truck and extra ovens to use for the day of the event. They also allowed us to return all unused, frozen pizzas. Unused milk and ice cream were donated to the children's preschool in our church. Many women volunteered to bake cookies and brownies as well.

Round tables were available in the Fellowship Hall for families to eat at. The entertainment committee scheduled many talented individuals from the church to appear on stage while people were eating. There was a variety of country western and bluegrass music, western dancers, puppetry, and mime.

A great number of people were required to keep the eating area stocked and clean. The kitchen crew was responsible for keeping food booths supplied with adequate amounts of food and beverages. Most of the hot food was prepared in the kitchen and carried to the appropriate booths as needed. Table-maintenance volunteers cleaned the tables routinely throughout the day. We were fortunate to have many young people from the church help us in this area. Also, bathrooms were checked hourly and kept clean and filled with supplies.

Because this event was an outreach, we staffed a table at the entrance of the gym with our women to answer questions and give out ministry information. This area also served as a lost and found and lost child area.

The Wild, Wild West Family Fun Day was held on the first Saturday in April from 10 AM to 6 PM. It was a great day of fun, food, fellowship, and entertainment for thousands attending and hundreds working. It surpassed all of our goals and made us realize that the Lord blesses us as we serve him and blesses those who participate as well.

PLANTING SEEDS WITH A CRAFT MINISTRY

Crafts can be a means of reaching friends for Christ and raising funds for missions. Do you have a friend who is turned off by the church but is turned on by crafts? Perhaps all is not lost. One important principle in reaching people with the gospel of Christ is to begin by establishing common interests. If your unbelieving friend is "crafty," and you are not, consider developing this interest in order to have fun with her and enjoy a new experience together. This will help establish one more common bond between the two of you.

Your Women's Ministries can assist you in leading your friend to Christ by creating a craft ministry. New and exciting classes can be offered at the conclusion of your women's Bible study or in homes. You may have a friend who would never set foot in a church except to work on crafts.

These classes could be offered weekly or monthly. Begin by asking some women who excel in craft-making in your church to donate their time and talents to teaching a series of craft classes. Become acquainted with the crafts to be taught, and design a brief devotional around each. For example, in a basket-weaving

One important principle in reaching people with the gospel of Christ is to begin by establishing common interests.

class you might speak on the threads that weave our lives together and how a basket of reeds cannot be woven together unless the reeds are first thoroughly soaked in water. Explain the similarities to our lives, how we often feel frayed, and our lives tend to come apart at the seams or lack symmetry. Explain that water is a biblical symbol of the Holy Spirit and that when we ask Christ into our hearts to be the Lord of our lives, we are filled with the Holy Spirit. Just as the water helps the reeds to bend and makes them pliable for weaving a lovely basket, so the Holy Spirit smooths the rough edges of our lives, tucks in the loose ends, and helps our hearts to become pliable, bending to the will of God. This process gradually conforms us to the image of Christ, which makes us lovely in God's eyes.

A devotional only needs to be three minutes long. It should be short and focused on the class. It is ideal to have the craft teacher present it as a natural part of her class. If she feels she is unable to, a helper could be assigned to give the devotional, pass out supplies, answer questions about the craft, and clean up.

The devotionals aren't designed to explain the gospel in its entirety. This is not their purpose. Rather, you are giving gold nuggets for your participants to mull over, to make them hungry for more. Your goal is to provide a context for evangelism. Afterward, some gentle questions to your friend might lead to a fuller discussion of the gospel.

Generally, a small donation is requested to cover the cost of the materials, and the women go home understanding how to make a new project. What happens to the craft? We ask everyone to donate the crafts to our annual Christmas program and craft fair. We explain that the proceeds from these crafts are divided and distributed among home and foreign missions. These beneficiaries are chosen early in the year by our women's ministries board so that they can be announced at the craft classes. Women like to know what they are giving to.

An inviting atmosphere is important for the craft classes. Warmly welcome the women and introduce friends who have been invited. Coffee and refreshments can help set the mood for a fun and cozy get-together. Naturally move right from the devotional into teaching the craft. Remember that the unbelieving visitors are far more significant than the crafts. You might even try adding an icebreaker to help women develop their friendships.

EVANGELISM TRAINING
ACROSS THE MINISTRIES

Hosting a seminar on evangelism can equip your Women's Ministries' participants and benefit your whole church. Our "Reaching Out" Conference was available to the entire congregation, and we strongly encouraged our women leaders to attend. We used this simple half-day format:

8:30 AM	Registration
8:45 AM	Welcome, Announcements, and Drama
9:00 AM	Keynote Message
9:45 AM	Break
9:55 AM	Seminars: Developing Your Skills
10:50 AM	Break
11:05 AM	Seminars: Applying Your Skills
12:00 PM	Lunch (optional)
1:00 PM	Open Air Evangelism (optional)
3:30 PM	Open Air Participants Return to Church

The keynote speaker addressed the topic "Communicating the Gospel." Participants then chose two seminars to attend. The seminar leaders were from our own church, lay people active in evangelism, on the pastoral staff, or in parachurch ministries.

The attendees received a list of upcoming evangelism opportunities and contacts for more information, and they also had a chance that very day to share the gospel with our optional Open Air Evangelism training and practicum. The Applying Your Skills seminar offered training during the morning. The participants actually organized an open air meeting which had been advertised beforehand in a nearby suburb. After brief testimonies and a gospel presentation, the Open Air students turned to people in the audience and drew them into conversations about the gospel.

An Evangelism Training Seminar offers an excellent method of periodic training which will boost the women and the church.

SEMINARS

Developing Your Skills

Communicating the Gospel

"Before we get the story out, we need to get the story straight!" In our desire to be more effective in sharing our faith we often overlook the need to know and understand the biblical content of the message which we want to communicate. This seminar will concentrate on the content of the gospel message.

Answering the Tough Questions

"I'm not so bad compared to everyone else." "This life is the only thing I'm sure of." "I stopped believing in God the day my brother died." This seminar will concentrate on the most common roadblocks to acceptance of Christ. We will discuss how we can understand what lies behind such tough questions and how we can begin to answer them.

Following Up New Christians

Do you have a friend who has recently expressed a deepening interest in spiritual things? Do you know how to meet her needs for basic information and direction as she begins a personal walk with the Lord? This seminar will help you formulate a plan to help equip your friend for service to the Lord.

Leading a Child to Christ

The evangelization of children is difficult because it requires the communication of complex theological truths in simple terms. This seminar will focus on what it means for a child to become a Christian and how to communicate the gospel in age-appropriate language.

Mobilizing Teens for Evangelism

This seminar will discuss why it is so difficult to mobilize today's youth for evangelism. It will give practical suggestions for overcoming these difficulties. A plan will be presented for preparing teens to witness and suggestions will be made on practical application of evangelism.

Applying Your Skills

Using Your Home for Evangelistic Bible Studies

The purpose of the seminar is to train lay men and women in the practical how-to's of leading an evangelistic Bible study in their own home. Inviting people, creating a warm atmosphere, and understanding group dynamics will be the focus of our discussion. We will be using *Examining the Claims of Jesus* (Fisherman Bible Study Guides) as an example of one approach to use in this context of ministry.

Evangelizing Through Sports

This seminar will explore the idea of how sports can be used to reach people for Christ. We will look at the biblical basis for using sports to evangelize, consider some benefits of using sports as a ministry tool, and talk about some practical how-to's, such as how we can use sports to create an attractive and effective environment for evangelism.

Reaching Your Sphere of Influence

This seminar will explore the why's and how-to's of evangelism as it pertains to ordinary people. We will present practical suggestions and approaches for sharing Christ at home, at work, and at play. Be prepared for some humor and personal interaction. We will discuss the difference between using Christ to increase your vocation and using your vocation to share Christ.

Evangelistic Parties for Kids

Sharing the Good News is an exciting opportunity to touch the lives of neighbor children ages three to eight for the Lord Jesus! We will discuss the message, the effective messenger, and the method.

How to Reach Friends at School

This seminar will focus on the idea of "Lifestyle Evangelism." It will discuss and help apply practical ways for teens to share their faith with their friends.

Open Air Evangelism

Do you feel like you have not challenged yourself lately? Need some practice communicating your faith? Dying for a chance to talk about something more significant than the weather yet never find anyone interested? Consider participating in Open Air Evangelism. We will demonstrate sketchboard evangelism and provide instruction for those who would like to be a part of it. If you like people and good conversations, please join us.

Perspective

Between Your Own Two Feet

As I lay in a hospital bed in Cambridge, England, I plied Janet, the young girl who had just led me to Christ, with questions. "What do you mean, 'share my faith?'" I asked. I was unchurched and totally ignorant of evangelical cliches.

"Tell your friends what's happened to you," she explained.

"Why?" I asked, astonished at the novel idea.

"So they can do what you've done," she replied.

"That's 'sharing my faith?'" I inquired.

"Yes, Jill, that's sharing your faith."

"But what if they ask me questions I can't answer?"

"Oh, they'll do that all right." Janet laughed. "Just tell them you'll find out the answers if you don't know them."

"But," I gasped, "where do I do that—find the answers?"

"Come and ask me," Janet instructed me, "and if I don't know the answer, I'll find out for you."

So went my first class on evangelism entitled, "Telling your friends." The workshop followed within two hours of this conversation, as my rowdy university friends clattered down the ward to visit me. My heart beating furiously, I tried to share my faith. As far as I could tell, nothing I said had any effect whatsoever, except to lose me my closest companions.

"What sort of friends are they if you tell them you've found God and they dump you?" Janet remarked after my sorrowful report.

"They are the only friends I've got," I remonstrated. "And they're good ones too. I don't want them to think I'm weird or something."

Back on the college campus, I discovered I was a missionary. I had never met a missionary and hadn't a clue as to the details of their occupation, but I entered into the next class on evangelism entitled, "The mission field is between your own two feet." My friends, like myself, though raised in so-called "Christian" England, were as biblically illiterate as I. They didn't know they were sinners, lost, and that Christ had died for them. No one had ever explained to them the personal application of the gospel account of the birth, life, death, and resurrection of Jesus. I sensed that, like myself, they had not really rejected Jesus—they just hadn't had a chance to receive him. I got to work and began to lead one after another to Christ.

I discovered that friendship came first. They were not going to listen to me if they didn't like me! Then, sharing my experience could come next, opening up an opportunity for questions. Sometimes I was able to explain the four steps to Christ that Janet had shared with me: the fact of sin, the penalty of sin, Christ's death for us, and finally, the need to accept him by his Holy Spirit into our life. Sometimes they weren't ready for this last step. I learned to be content to put my link on the chain and pray that the next Christian would add the next, until the final link was added. After all, even Paul said, "I planted the seed, Apollos watered it. . . ." Then the added clincher, "but God made it grow" (I Corinthians 3:6). All of us can have a part in someone's salvation. That's what evangelism is all about, but in the end, it is God who makes it happen.

But what about all those questions you might not know the answers to? I found I was very motivated to get into the Scriptures to find out! And so I began to grow, as I strove to keep a step or two ahead of the people God was using me to lead to him. As I looked around me, I was tempted to become very intimidated by strong Christians, girls older and a lot wiser than I was, with wonderful Christian backgrounds and a lifetime of teaching behind them. Most of the time I felt as if I was a very weak link in a very strong chain. But I came to understand that a weak link is better than no link, and even a weak link is vital.

Whatever evangelistic events we plan in our women's ministry, never forget personal evangelism needs to be going on moment by moment and day by day in all of our lives. This being the case, when the event comes along, we will not be scratching our heads, wondering whom to bring along. The measure of personal work going on through everyone in a ministry will, in the end, determine the success of the corporate event.

JILL BRISCOE

Chapter 14

Women on a Mission

Many women today are on a mission, although not necessarily the kind of mission that you can incorporate into your women's ministries program. What kind of mission, then, is practical for a ministry geared to women, most of whom have full-time responsibilities caring for their children or at work? How can missions be a vital part of a program that involves women from such a variety of backgrounds and situations?

When asking how missions can be incorporated into women's ministries, it is essential to see missions as more than simply a *part* of the ministry. Instead, missions should be the heartbeat. Under the umbrella of the Great Commission, a ministry of mission committed to the evangelization and discipleship of women is the building block of women's ministries. Those who birth a women's ministry within the context of a church are most likely motivated by a strong sense of mission and the desire to pursue the mission field in which they find themselves.

If the women of your women's ministries are concerned with reaching their own backyards with the gospel, they will also be excited about reaching backyards in Venezuela or Guatemala. A strong missions foundation for your program will manifest itself through tangible mission outreaches and opportunities. It is exciting to see new ministries and service projects spring up from within a ministry driven by the Great Commission.

Building upon a missions foundation involves teaching women the biblical concept of making disciples. First, Christians must real-

> A ministry of mission committed to the evangelization and discipleship of women is the building block of women's ministries.

ize that we are messengers of the good news for those who do not yet know. We are being saved so that we can share the gospel with others; we are promised hope of eternal life so that we can offer hope to a forlorn world; and we are promised God's provision so we can lay our lives down to meet the needs of others. A chosen generation is not chosen solely for its own benefit, but also for the benefit of others who may see the goodness of God through the lives of his children and believe and be saved.

So where does missions fit in the lives of busy women? Local outreach opportunities and cross-cultural experiences can be used to broaden women's view of the world and excite them about the opportunities to serve others through missions. You may want to work in conjunction with existing outreach centers in your community or tap into the missionary resources in other area churches, tailoring the opportunities you offer to the interests of your women.

The Women's Ministries of Elmbrook offer a variety of local outreaches according to the make-up of different groups. Each of the three ministries has a missions representative on its committee, and she is responsible to organize a missions committee to plan opportunities and to build a vision for missions within her ministry. Evening Edition, a ministry for working women, has used missionaries to help them link interested women to cross-cultural or social ministries within the community, even to ministries within a prison community. Moms and More aims to encourage those missionary moms who are in the field and also mothers in the inner city of Milwaukee. This is accomplished through baby showers, birthday parties for Jesus, and visits to a women's shelter. Morning Break has a yearly Missions Brunch that highlights a missions speaker and assigns each table a missionary. This branch of women's ministries also links up with the Milwaukee Rescue Mission's women's shelter, known as "Joy House."

CULTIVATING A MISSIONS VISION

Taking advantage of the church-wide missions emphasis will provide a natural springboard for cultivating a heart for missions in particular areas of ministry. The annual church Missions Festival at Elmbrook is unique in that almost every area of the church focuses its attention for one week on our missionaries, especially those who are home on furlough. The Women's Ministry

> **Local outreach opportunities and cross-cultural experiences can be used to broaden women's view of the world and excite them about the opportunities to serve others through missions.**

participates by hosting a Missions Brunch in place of its normally scheduled study. Each brunch table is matched with a missionary. This helps the women get to know a particular missionary better and increases their awareness of what God is doing in a particular part of the world. The focus of the program and the speaker is to expose women to the needs of a lost world, to educate women as to what God is doing around the world, and to motivate women to play an active role in fulfilling the Great Commission. During this week "missionary moms" are also interviewed at the Moms and More meetings. This helps women realize that although they may live worlds apart, their lives as young mothers are full of the same daily routines and struggles.

Catching the Vision

After the missions festival is over, the familiar routine settles in. The missionaries go back to the field. The passion and the realities of reaching the world for Christ seem to fit comfortably back into the map that hangs on the wall. During the week the women were able to catch a glimpse of the needs but did not experience cross-cultural missions first-hand. It is one thing to see a slide show and another to see a famished child; it's one thing to hear about the struggles of a missionary and another to experience the routine three-hour trip to the nearest grocery store; it's one thing to smell an international meal and another to smell the stench of a decaying city.

We decided that a helpful way of nurturing a vision for missions was to see, hear, and smell another culture first-hand. That way, we too can be touched, awakened, and moved for the sake of the gospel. You may already have incorporated a Missions Brunch, Missions Week, or an "Adopt-a-Missionary" month in your women's ministry program. There are a variety of ways to cultivate a missions vision at home, but what better way could there be than to take a group of key women to another country as cross-cultural workers? These women will then be able to inspire and motivate others, helping them to catch a vision as well.

Making the Vision a Reality

To give women an international missions experience, we began looking within our church family for missionaries to host our missions team. Two missionary women who were home on furlough

The church-wide missions emphasis will provide a natural springboard for cultivating a heart for missions in particular areas of ministry.

We decided that a helpful way of nurturing a vision for missions was to see, hear, and smell another culture first-hand.

To give women an international missions experience, we began looking within our church family for missionaries to host our missions team.

were asked if they would host a small team of women for a two-week vacation and exposure trip to their country of service. Bobbie Burns, a church planter from the city of Caracas, Venezuela, and Jana Price, a Bible translator working with an Indian tribe in Colorado Valley, Venezuela, both agreed. Each missionary was asked to draft a tentative, ten-day schedule for the trip, one that would give our women a taste of the culture while using them to serve the nationals and the missionaries at the same time.

As we began to move toward offering this international missions opportunity, we felt that it was necessary to define our goals clearly. We wanted everyone involved—those who were sending the team, the missionaries receiving the team, and the team itself—to understand the purpose of the trip clearly. Our Women's Ministries clarified that the purpose was primarily to expose women to another culture in order to help build a vision for missions at home. Thus we named them "Vacations with a Vision." Here is the statement of purposes we drafted.

Women's Ministries "Vacation with a Vision" Mission Statement

Our Women's Ministries clarified that the purpose was primarily to expose women to another culture in order to help build a vision for missions at home.

- To build a missions vision within the women's ministries
- To expose women to the needs and realities of Elmbrook missionaries
- To broaden one's Christian world view so that it includes cross-cultural missions
- To understand the realities of the Great Commission by seeing what God is doing in the world
- To experience cross-cultural ministry

PLANNING AHEAD

After communicating these purposes to the missionaries, we agreed to tentative dates for our trips, a year in advance, and set the amount of time and number of meetings needed to prepare. Since our missionaries would be on furlough for the initial four months of planning, we decided to organize our teams early so that the missionary women could get acquainted with those women who would be "on vacation" with them. It was necessary to determine the number that each missionary could handle, the approximate cost of the trip, the tentative schedule, and what kind of application procedure was needed to select the teams. We held a meeting for anyone interested that supplied all the necessary information. The following sheet was provided:

Women's Ministry "Vacation with a Vision" Information Sheet

Who:

Those women who desire to build a vision for missions personally and within the Women's Ministries through first-hand, cross-cultural experience, and who want to be a means for others to catch the vision as well.

What:

Two "Vacation with a Vision" Opportunities

Where and When:

1. Caracas, Venezuela with Bobbi Burns
   January 1995 (two weeks)
   Five to six approximate openings
   Cost: $1,000 (may vary)
   Opportunity for exposure to city ministry and surrounding areas.
2. Colorado Valley, Venezuela with Jana Price
   January 1995 (two weeks)
   Eight approximate openings
   Cost: $1,000 (may vary)
   Tribal setting provides opportunity for work projects, cooking, typing, and painting, sharing of testimonies, visiting Indian villages, and traveling.

How:

We will not be receiving financial support from Women's Ministries as these are "vacations" and are specifically planned as vision-building trips. You will be sending prayer letters and may also ask friends for financial support.

COMMUNICATING THE VISION

Presenting these missions opportunities to the women in your ministry takes strategy. We first introduced our formal game plan to the steering committee. This group consists of all ministry coordinators whose key roles demanded being well-informed of our plans. Next we sent special invitations to all ministry coordinators, small-group teachers and shepherds, doulas, and committee leaders, with the purpose of encouraging participation from those who have demonstrated leadership and commitment to the ministry. Then in the two months prior to the informational meeting, we announced an informational meeting in all of the weekly programs at least two or three times.

Application Procedures

Our missionaries communicated various concerns and problems that they had experienced with short-term teams in the past, especially in the areas of team-building and unity. They were very helpful in giving us specific questions to ask on the application. The missionaries wanted to understand what motivations and expectations the participants would have, both before and during the trip. The application was helpful to the selection committee as well as the missionaries. Responses provided information on various life issues of those interested. The missionaries could see the applicant's goals and hopes for their experience and the testimony helped them know how they could pray for those women selected for the teams. The application also gave each woman the opportunity to look carefully into different areas of her life to see what God was teaching and what areas needed his attention.

After talking with many who applied, checking references, and reviewing the applications with the missionaries, the women were selected and notified of their acceptance on the team. The missionaries were somewhat concered that some of the women had unrealistic expectations about what they could accomplish on the field because language and cultural barriers often prevent short-termers from doing a great deal of personal ministry. The missionaries addressed such issues in training sessions.

Preparation

After the teams are organized and the women are notified, the preparation begins! Addressing physical, spiritual, and emotional issues is essential during the months of preparation. Three topics were discussed while our missionaries were still on furlough: a "Biblical Basis for Missions," "Team Building," and "Spiritual Warfare."

Your first meetings should highlight the general expectations and game plan for the months ahead. These are key times for the teams to get to know the missionaries and learn about the field they will be visiting. Learning how to prepare a prayer/support letter is important, as many women will be concerned about this from the beginning. They should be sent out at least two months prior to the trip. It is essential to form prayer teams that will undergird your trips with prayer. Women on the team can be paired as prayer partners, and other women in your women's group will want to pray for specific women on the mission's team as well.

Soon the team members should begin sharing their testimonies with each other as a way for them to get to know each other. Many mental and physical games and activities can be used to promote team building, such as survival list games and ropes courses. A psychological testing approach would help to identify leadership traits and allow the women the opportunity to discuss how they work together in a team.

Further Preparation

Culture Shock

One of the missionaries was very concerned about the issue of control. She wanted each of the women to understand where they stood on a spectrum of needing to control or be controlled. Because, in America, we are so used to having tremendous control over every decision in our lives, it is difficult to assess how one will respond in a situation where most controls are taken away. This is just one area of culture shock that the missionaries could address with those on their team.

Passports/Immunization

Applying for passports and obtaining immunizations should be done well in advance. Travel agencies usually have a listing of the immunizations necessary for most countries.

Safety Issues

Safety issues related to money and ethnic foods are important to examine according to the area where you will be going. It may

Addressing physical, spiritual, and emotional issues is essential during the months of preparation.

be helpful for the missionaries to write a list of do's and don't's that would apply specifically to their area.

Packing Tips

The best tip I received was, "Pack your bags and then take out half of that!" Here again, ask your missionary what you will need and write a list for her team. Keep in mind that room in your team's suitcases may be needed to take items for the missionaries that they cannot obtain or clothing for nationals. Check with airlines regarding weight limits and international regulations.

RETURNING AND COMMUNICATING THE VISION

Before what is out of sight becomes out of mind, decide how your team can communicate what they have learned to the rest of the women's group. Designing a plan before you leave is the first step toward building a vision when you return. Each member of your team could choose a different way to express what she has experienced. Following are a variety of ways your women can communicate all they have seen and learned. Note how you can plan your method for communicating your vision before you leave.

Personal Testimony

Bring an extra journal or notebook to record your daily reflections. Try to capture the smells, sights, and tastes. As you experience a new culture, keep in mind the perspective of those who are not there. Ask yourself, "What looks and smells different? What are some food items or types of housing that I have never seen before?"

Slides and Video

Watching missionary slide shows before you go is very helpful. Write down what kind of slides or video portions interested you the most. Perhaps you were drawn to people, rather than the scenery, but do include both. In video and slide presentation it is helpful to begin with the big picture. Then move to the more specific as you focus on the city or town; then narrow in on the lives of the missionaries and those with whom they work. What daily routines fill their day? What is their church life like? Purchase film according to the typical weather expected in the area at the time you will be going. Ask about film in camera

"Pack your bags and then take out half of that!"

Bring an extra journal or notebook to record your daily reflections.

stores and make sure your camera or video recorder is in good working order before you go. There is nothing like shooting five rolls of film only to find out that your shutter was not working properly!

Ethnic Night

Those with an interest in cooking might focus on the recipes of the missionaries and stick around the kitchen to pick up a few tips. Bring recipe cards and conversion charts, depending on the areas of the world to which you go. A cookbook with a pictorial description of herbs, vegetables, fruits, and greens may help identify uncertain foods. Hosting dinners with those women in your small group upon return will add flavor as you communicate your experiences.

Some women may nurture a ministry vision by writing music, sketching or painting, or writing a poem. Others whose lives have been changed by their experience will communicate their new excitement for missions spontaneously, with no planning at all! In whatever way a team chooses to communicate their experiences, it is exciting to know that their lives will never be the same. They will look at their world through new eyes.

After the stories are told and the slides presented, you may want to start from the beginning and make plans for the next year. Standing behind your missionaries in sending short-term and career missionaries to the field will be exciting fruits of these vacations. As you keep in mind the plentiful needs of the harvest, continue as God leads you to raise up laborers for the fields.

Some women may nurture a ministry vision by writing music, sketching or painting, or writing a poem.

Standing behind your missionaries in sending short-term and career missionaries to the field will be exciting fruits of these vacations.

RECOMMENDED READING LIST

Borthwick, Paul. *A Mind for Missions*. Colorado Springs: NavPress, 1987.

Bryant, David. *In the Gap*. Downers Grove, Ill.: InterVarsity Press, 1979.

Hybels, Bill. *Honest to God?* Grand Rapids: Zondervan, 1990.

Elliot, Elizabeth. *No Graven Image*. 1966; repr., Westchester, Ill.: Crossway, 1982.

_____. *Shadow of the Almighty*. 1958; repr., New York: HarperCollins, 1989.

_____. *Through Gates of Splendor*. 1970; rev. ed., Wheaton, Ill.: Tyndale House, 1986.

Kane, J. Herbert. *The Making of a Missionary.* Grand Rapids: Baker, 1975.

Purnell, Dick. *Building Relationships That Last.* Arrowhead Springs, Calif.: Here's Life Publishers, 1988.

Richardson, Don. *Peace Child.* Glendale, Calif.: Regal Books, 1974.

Tucker, Ruth. *From Jerusalem to Irian Jaya.* Grand Rapids: Zondervan, 1983.

White, John. *The Fight.* Downers Grove, Ill.: InterVarsity Press, 1976.

Wilson, Sam, and Gordon Aeschliman. *The Hidden Half: Discovering the World of Unreached Peoples.* Monrovia, Calif.: World Vision International, 1984.

World Christian Magazine. P.O. Box 40010, Pasadena, CA 91104.

Part V

ENERGIZING YOUR MINISTRY

Chapter 15

Being Women
of Prayer

"*Cling. . . .*" *This simple* word evokes visions of a small child, tears streaming down her face, running into the arms of a loving parent and burying her tiny face into safe, warm arms. It brings to mind a hundred love stories, true and make-believe, of couples holding fast to each other and their commitment of love. Do we contemplate our relationship with the Almighty God in these same ways, as passionate devotion or a loving hug, or does that kind of intimacy seem strange and incomprehensible? Yet the Scriptures instruct us to have an intimate communion with God. In addition to serving him (we know how to do that), and fearing him (perhaps we are even better at this), and keeping his commandments (oh, yes, we understand that), we are told to listen to his voice ". . . and cling to Him."

The word *cling* in the original Hebrew refers to a connection as close as our bones are to our skin! It is the same word used in Genesis 2:24 when God describes the one-flesh bond in marriage. It connotes not only physical proximity, but also loyalty and affection. It means sticking to, remaining in, and being lovingly joined.

What an incredible picture of commitment and protection, a sanctuary of love. Not only is such closeness presented as a pos-

You shall follow the Lord your God and fear Him; and you shall keep His commandments, listen to His voice, serve Him, and cling to Him.

—Deuteronomy 13:4, NASB

sibility; it is stated as a commandment to us. The reality can be ours. We cling to God when we follow his commandments, serve him, fear him, and enter a saving relationship with his son, Jesus. And we cling to God by endeavoring to maintain an intimate, communicative relationship with him through prayer. This is how we listen for his voice, and this is how we talk to him. Prayer is key to knowing, loving, and clinging to God.

WHY WE PRAY

Imagine a family in which no one talks to each other. Or a telephone conversation between two friends in which only one person ever speaks. Imagine an engaged couple that never talks excitedly about their approaching wedding day. Each example sounds silly and empty because it is only natural that there should be active and engaging conversations between people in loving, committed relationships. Now think about our relationship with God—by far the most genuine, trustworthy, committed, and long-lasting relationship we can ever know. Shouldn't our greatest joy be in speaking to him and listening to his heart?

Of course the answer is yes. But for many of us, our experience falls short of our expectation. Perhaps we are approaching prayer in the wrong way, or our expectations are misdirected. Prayer is often misunderstood as the vehicle for receiving our desires, rather than the means of discovering God's desires. But true prayer is coming face to face with the heart of the living God! It is learning how to communicate spirit-to-Spirit. It is one of the most integral ways in which God unleashes his power through his people, strengthens his church, affects change in a pagan world, and draws us nearer to himself for deepened communion.

For these reasons, prayer deserves to be both a discipline and a lifestyle. Every key leader in Scripture prayed. If that is not enough incentive, consider this: Jesus prayed, frequently and fervently. Prayer is commanded, encouraged, exalted, and cherished. Prayer is incredibly important.

Women in ministry need prayer. And women's ministries need prayer. You as a women's ministry leader need prayer for yourself and the ministry God has entrusted to you. And you need to teach your women about prayer. The impact of your current ministry can be greatly strengthened through more frequent and fervent prayer.

> **Prayer is often misunderstood as the vehicle for receiving our desires, rather than the means of discovering God's desires.**

RETHINKING PRAYER

Stop for a moment, and just think about prayer. Most of us were taught a simple model. Folded hands and a bowed head signaled the start of prayer. Then there were the very holy and churchy-sounding beginnings, followed by a few main requests, perhaps a thank you, and then a firm "amen." In light of this stark model, it is not too hard to fathom why many have considered prayer a chore, but, clearly, prayer was designed to be so much more than a formula. Prayer was designed by God to include worship, singing, talking, quiet loving, comforting reassurance, honest and open confession, and silent adoration.

If you had an incredibly good morning and a dear friend walked in your office, would you not want to share the entire experience with her in great detail? Think how your voice would sound as you spoke. Would it sound strained or artificial? Most likely it would be very expressive and full of emotion. Now think about how you talk to God. If you can identify a vast difference, you might want to reevaluate your approach to prayer. Without sacrificing reverence, we can talk to God in a manner that is straight-forward and natural. God knows us so well. There is no need to act stilted or artificial in his presence. As we think about prayer, we must be aware of our tendencies to become stale or synthetic. Reviewing the scriptural pictures of God's intimacy and his desire for us to listen and cling to him will help guide our words and approach to prayer. Before teaching others about prayer, we must first experience prayer as it was designed. Try to answer these questions thoughtfully:

The way to raise up praying women is by making leaders into women of prayer.

1. Why is prayer important?
2. What should prayer look like and sound like?
3. Why is intimacy with God a proper goal to establish in our hearts before we pray?

PRAYING AS LEADERS . . . IN PRIVATE

As we grow in our own understanding and personal practice of prayer, we can more effectively lead others in the joy and discipline of prayer. But this practice must begin in our own prayer closets. The way to raise up praying women is by making leaders into women of prayer. How much more effectively and honestly will we be able to preach about the benefits and necessity of prayer when we ourselves have experienced its value and urgency.

Therefore, make a commitment to yourself, the Lord, and your women to pray in private and make prayer a priority in your life. Find the peace that comes only from sitting at his feet in silent adoration. Notice your conviction deepen concerning the powerful advantages of prayer as you evidence God's response to it. Sense the increase in your own confidence and abilities as you seek his anointing for his work. Grow in your awareness of his voice as the Spirit guides, speaks, comforts, challenges, and convicts. Relish the times of personal worship in which your heart softens and your eyes well up with tears of joy as you are reacquainted and refreshed with the passion of first love for Jesus.

As you pray privately, make sure the following components are a part of your prayer life.

Praise and Worship

Spend time just loving your God and telling him so. Ask him to increase the passion of your love for his Son, and openly yield yourself to the fullness of the Holy Spirit. You may wish to sing, journal a love letter, read Scripture, meditate, or simply be still in his presence.

Confession

Examine your heart, motives, activities, plans, relationships with others and God, and ask the Lord to reveal areas of sin and weakness. Allow yourself to grieve over sin and to experience some of the pain that God feels over sin in his world. Accept his forgiveness and truly leave the guilt at the cross, so that you are renewed and cleansed.

Intercession

This important part of prayer should be more than a shopping list of wants. Rather, it is a way to be involved in God's work in the lives of others. It is praying for his will to be done, asking for his plans to be made clear and for our obedience to those plans, rebuking the enemy from gaining ground, and seeking God's empowerment in our lives. Use this time to discuss the needs of your women and ministry and pray for God's guidance. A prayer schedule categorizing specific needs on certain days can be helpful; but don't feel tied to an agenda. Allow the Spirit to prompt you to pray for people by listening for his leading.

Thanksgiving

Acknowledging God's goodness is essential to the heart of prayer and worship. By giving thanks we increase our faith for what God has done and heighten our anticipation for what he has in store for the future. We thank him because he deserves our appreciation, but in the process we find ourselves doubly blessed by recognizing that we are the object of his love and giving!

Fasting

You may want to occasionally (weekly, monthly, or at special times) fast for yourself, your women, and the ministry. Fasting helps us recognize God's strength in our weakness and pulls our attention away from daily needs and onto God's sustenance and provision. A full-day or half-day fast can be strategic in disengaging Satan's power in a particular area, furthering God's work in your ministry, discerning his will, or in focusing yourself more intently on the Lord in love and worship.

Personal Retreat Day

Three or four times per year escape from your daily responsibilities and plan a complete prayer day alone with the Lord. You may want to use devotional materials or simply allow the Spirit to guide your activities for that day. Incorporate meditation, Scripture reading, and all of the components of prayer, allowing God to revitalize and refresh your heart and mind as you spend time in his presence. Be sure not to use this as a study or work day, and if you choose to preset an agenda, be careful not to pack it too tightly.

If your prayer times incorporate these elements, along with a heart that is willing to embrace the person of God, you will find yourself delighting in prayer. Not only that, but you will walk away from times of prayer more ready to go forth and minister in power and partnership with the Father.

PRAYING AS LEADERS . . . IN PUBLIC

Since ministry leaders are often called upon to pray in public, they have the unique opportunity to teach about prayer through modeling. When Jesus raised Lazarus from the dead, he purposely prayed a public prayer of thanks to the Father, so that the work of God in response to prayer would be recognized (John 11:41–42).

We should not assume that our listeners know how to pray. Instead, we should frequently teach about prayer and what it means to talk to and listen to God. We should also display different styles of prayer such as

Since ministry leaders are often called upon to pray in public, they have the unique opportunity to teach about prayer through modeling.

- Silently listening for God's voice (Psalm 62:1, 5)
- Praying aloud with hands raised (Hebrews 5:7; 1 Timothy 2:8)
- Rejoicing in worship (Psalm 9:2)
- Kneeling (Ezra 9:5)
- Praying with others (Matthew 18:20)

Typically a leader praying in public prays from the front, out loud, while everyone silently prays along. But why not increase the involvement of others by creating opportunities for interjection and response? Here are a couple of examples:

1. Alphabetic Prayer—This helpful model can be used as an icebreaker or prayer starter. Beginning with the letter "A," ask your women to think of words that start with A that describe God's attributes. Possible answers might be "Awesome," "Almighty," and "Abba-Father." Encourage each woman who calls out an answer to turn it into a short prayer. Thus, the first response might go something like this:

Awesome. Your creation is awesome, God. I love to watch you paint sunsets and know that every element of nature is designed by you and sustained by your power. Thank you for who you are. Amen.

2. Testimonial Prayer—Select a topic, such as God's faithfulness, and invite women to offer prayer out of their own experiences. You may wish to open and close this prayer time if you have set time constraints.

Whatever way your women are used to praying—try teaching them a new way. Encourage variety, spontaneity, and personal expression in prayer. This will help keep prayer fresh and natural and demonstrate that God is a person with whom we can communicate individually and creatively.

LEADING OTHERS TO PRAY

As you grow in your own personal commitment to and practice of prayer, you will become increasingly aware of the need to lead and encourage your women to embrace prayer. You will want them to develop deeper personal prayer times and place prayer at the heart of their service to the Lord. Following are some practical ways you can implement prayer into the life of your women's ministry.

Prayer Chain

One of the easiest prayer programs to begin and maintain, the prayer chain teaches about prayer while it faithfully traces its results. A prayer chain is simply fashioned by providing a roster of names and telephone numbers and requesting a commitment to communicate prayer needs and praises through that list. Here are the steps necessary to starting a prayer chain:

1. Form a group of women who will commit to being part of a prayer chain. Keeping the chain a manageable size (five to ten people works well) aids in its effectiveness and helps create a sense of greater connectedness between the women.
2. Provide each woman with the names and telephone numbers of her prayer chain.
3. Assign a captain for each prayer chain.
4. Make requests as brief as possible, using only first names. Example: Sue, unsaved, two year old son, surgery.
5. Pass the need or praise down the chain. When a request is received, pray immediately over the phone. Then call the next person on the chain. Prayer captains communicate the need to other prayer captains who in turn pass the need down their chains.
6. Keep all needs confidential, and do not gossip.
7. Remember to communicate praises for answered prayer in the same way, so that God may be further glorified and your women may observe him working.

One final note on prayer chains—the goal is not to see how many people we can get praying for a particular need. God is not moved by some lofty, numeric target; rather, he delights in seeing his church united for his purposes. The chief end of intercession is that it ties Christian hearts together in love and concern for one another and fixes our attention on the One who sovereignly supplies all our needs.

> The chief end of intercession is that it ties Christian hearts together in love and concern for one another and fixes our attention on the One who sovereignly supplies all our needs.

Prayer Request Box

Placing a box for prayer requests in an accessible place provides a means for women to express their needs and allows the leaders of the women's ministry to pray for its members. Requests can either be prayed for by a small, responsible group, or sent down the individual prayer chains.

Prayer Calendar

One effective prayer tool is a calendar that outlines specific needs to be prayed for each day of the month. You may wish to photocopy a calendar with stated needs, or provide a blank calendar and ask your women to write in the needs they pray for daily.

Prayer Partners

A similar but more concise form of the prayer chain, prayer partners can be formed at any juncture (perhaps at the start of a new year or season) and sustained for long or short time periods. Prayer partners agree to pray faithfully for each other on an ongoing basis, as well as being more specifically available through times of crisis or need. Try partnering women at your next group Bible study and maintain the prayer relationship just until the next meeting. Then elicit testimonies from your women concerning the experience by asking questions such as, "How did it feel to be cared for in this special way?" The results will likely inspire your women and confirm the effectiveness and power of this approach.

Evening of Prayer

Once a month or quarter host a special evening of prayer for your ministry leaders at a private home. Send out an invitation and ask each woman to bring along an item for prayer. Begin with refreshments and a half-hour of fellowship. Then plan for an hour of prayer, changing the topic every five minutes or so. You may wish to use a local newspaper, church bulletin, or simply the items for prayer that your leaders have brought. End with prayer for the ministry and each others' families. You will build closeness and a deeper sense of Christ's body if the group meets regularly.

Special Events Prayer

To ensure that your conferences, retreats, or other special events are covered in prayer, form prayer committees to provide ongoing prayer support. A special events prayer committee should be coordinated as soon as possible after the idea for an event is conceived, and maintained through the course of the event. This committee can function as a prayer chain for members of other committees and might act as a teaching resource at the event. At our annual Breakaway, the prayer committee members assist spiritual counselors by praying with women in need. They also coordinated a special prayer breakfast prior to the event.

Prayer Concert

Consider hosting an annual prayer concert to teach and inspire your women about prayer and bring together a united heart of prayer to God. A prayer concert is simply an extended time of group prayer with a particular focus. For instance, plan a concert around the theme of revival. Here is a sample schedule:

7:00 PM	Prayer-worship leader welcomes guests, explains the agenda, and leads in opening prayer, asking the Holy Spirit to be present and guide the evening
7:05 PM	Singing (a medley of hymns and praise songs)
7:25 PM	Teaching on biblical basis for prayer, revival
7:30 PM	Presenting historical precedence for church revivals
7:35 PM	Time of repentance (quiet confession and meditation, followed by inviting individual guests to stand and pray)
7:45 PM	Time of restoration (Prayer-worship leader assures forgiveness; leads in praise singing)

8:00 PM	Prayer for our country, the unsaved (in small groups of four to five)
8:15 PM	Prayer for our church (in small groups of four to five)
8:30 PM	Prayer for God's renewal, revival (as a large group, allowing for singing, praising, or prophecy)
9:00 PM	End prayer concert

(For more information, see *Concerts of Prayer* by David Bryant, Regal Books, 1984.)

Prayer Summit

The 1990s have seen a surge of prayer summits throughout North America. The classic prayer summit brings together ministry leaders from differing walks of life (such as pastors throughout a metropolitan city), but may be easily adapted to your women's group. Begin by thinking of a retreat, but keep the focus strictly on prayer and worship, with the goal being Christian unity and spiritual revival. The prayer summit occurs off-site (hotel, conference center), establishes only a loose agenda, and typically takes place over a period of three to four days. (For more information, see *Prayer Summits* by Joe Aldrich, Multnomah Press, 1992.)

EVANGELISTIC PRAYER

As we grow in intimacy with God through prayer, our hearts will naturally ache for the many who have yet to know him. Prayer is a strong tool for evangelism in the hands and hearts of our women. Certainly you will be teaching your women to intercede for others in their prayers, but there are some specific prayer strategies you may wish to employ in the area of evangelism as well.

Prayer Triplets

This approach was made famous by the Church of the Open Door in California but has gained great popularity throughout the country. The design is simple: Team up three women (a triplet) to pray for three nonbelievers each (a total of nine) on an ongoing basis, with the goal being salvation for all nine. Triplets have been extremely successful, as God has honored the prayers of these dedicated teams.

> **Prayer is a strong tool for evangelism in the hands and hearts of our women.**

Prayer Walks

Our social concerns pastor recently teamed up with several other church pastors to pray for a three-hundred-square-block area of Milwaukee's central city. Named "Operation Jericho," the goal of this venture was to develop "Rahab Houses" (places of safety and Bible study) throughout this area and raise up a solid Christian contingency in this crime-ridden section of town. Before the door-to-door evangelism began, five months of intense prayer and prayer walks were first implemented. The Operation Jericho team walked up and down the streets gaining a close-up perspective and deepened heart-knowledge of the people and area which they were daily bringing before the Lord in prayer. As they walked they prayed that, like the city of Jericho, God would tear down the walls that divide people and break through to the souls that so needed to know his love. They sought to tear down the stronghold of Satan on this area and to create openness for God's people to come in. The prayer walks were very effective. More than two hundred Rahab houses were formed with an initial commitment to host weekly Bible studies.

You can adapt this strategy to your ministry by targeting a section of the city, perhaps a one-mile radius around your church, and beginning faithful prayer walks with your women. Plan a Saturday prayer walk from nine to eleven in the morning. If neighbors make curious inquiries, it is a great opportunity to talk about Christ!

Praying With Maps

A systematic way to pray for your city, neighborhood, or subdivision is to utilize a map. Available through your local municipal body, maps can be prayed through, street by street, over a fairly short period of time. The benefit of working with a map is that it can be done from home at anytime. Imagine the street as best as you can, filled with houses, families, businesses, and pray for those who work and live on that block. (Obviously the better you know your city, the easier this will be.) Use a yellow highlighter to mark off the streets already prayed for. One family found this an exceptionally good way to get to know their neighbors, as they began praying through their subdivision directory.

MAINTAINING YOUR RELATIONSHIP

In 1 Thessalonians 5:17, the apostle Paul declares that we should pray "without ceasing." To accomplish this, we must have an ongoing focus on the work of God, as well as an unending relational connection with the person of God. Our relationship with the Father began before he created us (Psalm 139:16), was restored through Christ (Romans 5:1), and now is sustained through the Holy Spirit's power and living residence in our earthly bodies (Romans 8:11). As Jesus lives evermore to intercede for us (Hebrews 7:25), so also we have been given a ministry to intercede for others (James 5:16), and to be a model of Christ's dependent, passionate, and communicative relationship with the Father (Matthew 26:36–46).

Prayer binds us together with the Lord and one another. Prayer develops the relationship we are to enjoy with the living God, and teaches us to draw on his power and will to accomplish what he has established for our lives. Prayer refreshes our souls with the comfort and certainty of his presence. And prayer moves the heart of God in loving response to the petitions and needs of his people.

We hope this chapter has inspired and motivated you with creative ways to make prayer a priority in your own life and more central in the life of your women's ministry. If so, it achieved its purpose. But now the fun and excitement really starts. . . . Are you ready to begin praying?

Epilogue

Women Who Change Their World

Women who change their world are women whom God can use. And the women whom God can use are women with a heart for him and a calling to care for, nurture, and reach their own. As surely as God calls men and women to people groups in Africa, Asia, or Europe, I believe God calls women to women's ministry in their own communities. As I have met such women literally around the world, I have been impressed by common elements among them.

First, women are a *priority* in these women's lives. It is hard to figure out which priority comes first, but such a calling involves an absorption with women's needs that spills over into domestic duties and finds them awake in the middle of the night working out ways to do the job better.

Second, there is a *prayer ministry* for women in these women's lives that underlies all they do. I have sat in a hut in rural Laos and listened to a missionary pray her heart out for the women of her country; I have joined in the heartrending prayers of a pastor's wife who has suffered dreadfully in Croatia for women refugees like her; and I have been greatly moved by the tears of an Indian sister who, out of her own burning desire to serve women, has been used of God to mobilize more than three thousand women in prayer groups across her vast and needy country. If we are to be used of God among women, we will have a prayer power that drives us to our knees.

Third, I have observed that women greatly used of God to minister to other women have a *passion* for their work. They are driven to rise early and retire late, pushing the boundaries in order to see God's kingdom come among women. Theirs is no half-hearted effort to drum up some sort of enthusiasm for a project they had foisted on them. Theirs is no false joy. They love what they do and are always thirsty for more. What's more, they talk incessantly about it; their enthusiasm is contagious.

Last, they find *pleasure* in all they do and particularly take delight in the women themselves. Like a mother who believes her plain child is beautiful, I have heard many a woman brag about a woman in her group or on her committee as if she were a favorite child. What joy! And this joy transcends most of the fatigue, pressures, and stress that inevitably accompany women's ministry. There is, after all, the incredible and unique joy of finding and doing God's will; nothing compares with that. It has been my experience, as I know it has been Laurie's and Beth's, to embrace this kind of high and holy calling to serve women.

We pray that this book will not be a sterile manual that you feel you "must" read to get a job done, but rather that you may find yourselves glad for another tool to better equip yourselves for love and laughter in a life of women's ministry. When God calls you, you will know that women are a priority, drive your prayers, light a passionate fire for action, and give you eternal pleasure. You will not find yourself asking God, "Must I do this?" but "May I!" May the Lord find us faithful to his call as we reach a world of women waiting for someone to love them for him.

—JILL BRISCOE

Appendix 1

❧

CARING FOR A SPEAKER

The success of an event or program often rests with the speaker. Obviously, the speaker should be an appropriate person for the event. But the success of the speaker often depends on the quality of the arrangements made in her behalf. A group that understands well the care and handling of speakers will reap many benefits for the ministry. Not the least is that speakers will welcome a return invitation, and other speakers will discover by word of mouth that your group is on the ball.

The following are some suggestions for helping your group secure the speakers it wants and making them feel at home. These apply to plenary speakers, adjunct speakers, seminar leaders, and workshop facilitators.

A. Before the Invitation
  1. Decide honorariums or fees to be awarded
  2. Appoint a speaker-contact chairperson
    a. This will be the *one* person authorized to call or correspond with the speaker
    b. All correspondence should be filed for reference
  3. Determine the kind of speaker best suited to the program
  4. Obtain references or tapes of potential speakers

B. The Invitation
  1. Be specific!
  2. Plan to contact a well-known person one-to-two years in advance
    a. The first contact with the speaker or the speaker's secretary will be to confirm availability for the intended date of the program
    b. Obtain verbal acceptance of the invitation
  3. A prompt letter should follow that fulfills several objectives:
    a. Confirms the dates
    b. States primary considerations: the purpose of the event, its location, the time span, the number of times the person is expected to speak
    c. Describes secondary considerations: length of presentations, type of audience and anticipated number, sponsoring group, accommodations, travel arrangements, and remuneration plans

        d. Includes a doctrinal statement and speaker guidelines if the group has them

    4. Requests a doctrinal statement of faith or agreement from the invitee

    5. Requests a biography and picture appropriate for publicity

    6. Provides the name and telephone number of the contact chairperson

C. Before the Event

  After the speaker has been confirmed:

    1. Send a copy of all printed promotional materials to the speaker

    2. Update the speaker of any changes from the original invitation

    3. Arrange and pay for transportation, including all air travel

    4. Provide a map and directions to the facility if the speaker is driving

    5. Inquire whether the speaker will bring a guest

        a. More appropriate if the speaker is driving

        b. Cost of air travel discourages bringing a guest

    6. Inquire about special needs: type of microphone, overhead projector, handouts, book handling, taping policy, special dietary needs, rest

    7. Contact a few days before the event to be sure all details have been covered

    8. Assign speaker an on-site hostess or shepherd

    9. Advise the speaker who will be meeting her and who the hostess is

   10. Pray for the speaker and encourage her

D. During the Event

  Responsibilities of the hostess or shepherd

    1. Provide transportation from and to the airport and during the event

    2. Determine a rendezvous point for a speaker arriving by car

    3. Have program materials on hand and review the program with the speaker

    4. Help the speaker keep to the time schedule

    5. Usher the speaker to the assigned locations at the facility and elsewhere

    6. See to practical requests: dietary needs, rest, prayer, study time, water at the podium

E. Follow-up

    1. Send a prompt thank-you note with the remuneration

    2. If evaluations were received, relate to the speaker some personal comments and compliments

    3. Return publicity photographs

Appendix 2

SURVEYS AND FORMS

This appendix contains some of Elmbrook Women's Ministries' basic surveys and forms, which can be adapted for your specific purposes. We hope they will help you save time and energy in preparing instruments that will be effective for your ministries.

MOMS AND MORE PROFILE AND PARTNERSHIP SURVEY

YOUR PROFILE

Name_____ Home Phone_____ Work Phone_____

Your age_____ Ages of your children_____

Your church affiliation_____

1. How long have you been attending Moms and More? (Count this year as one year.) _____

2. How did you become interested in Moms and More? (You may choose more than one response.)
   - ❑ A friend
   - ❑ Church bulletin
   - ❑ Special event (e.g., Brunch, Birthday Party for Jesus)
   - ❑ Other (please explain)
   _____
   _____
   _____

3. Do you currently attend:
   ❑ Speaker weeks   ❑ Bible study weeks   ❑ Both

4. Are you currently involved in any of these women's ministries?
   ❑ Morning Break   ❑ Evening Edition   ❑ Bridges   ❑ Widow's Might

5. Please list your current or past areas of service and/or participation at your church:
   _____
   _____
   _____

6. Please check all items that apply:
   - ❑ I am a mom at home full-time
   - ❑ I am a single mom (check one):
     ❑ separated   ❑ divorced   ❑ widowed
   - ❑ I am a mom working outside the home. My work hours are: _____
   - ❑ I have a paid job out of my home

7. Please list your college major(s) or areas of special training:
   _____
   _____
   _____
   _____

8. Please list your special abilities, talents, hobbies, work experiences, etc.:
   _____
   _____
   _____
   _____

YOUR SERVICE

The rest of the survey will proceed from needs in specific areas to general needs that may be shared by more than one area. If you desire to serve with the Moms and More ministry, please check your area(s) of interest.

Bible Study

____ Teacher

____ Shepherd

____ Doula

____ Teacher-in-training (paired with an experienced teacher)

____ Administrative assistant (putting out table tents, checking on room setups, phone calling, etc.)

Children's Area

____ Room mom

____ Paid worker (must be able to sign Elmbrook Church's Statement of Faith)

____ Substitute paid worker

____ Host for paid worker coffees once a month, 8:15–8:45 AM

Hospitality

____ Prepare hospitality table

____ Greet newcomers

____ Assist newcomers for a few weeks, as needed

____ Call newcomers for follow-up

____ Prepare permanent name tags (summer only)

Hostessing

____ Make coffee and set up refreshment table, have nursery available at 8:45 AM

____ Clean up kitchen and refreshment table

____ Make a special table arrangement for a theme day

____ Make a special treat for a theme day

Missions

____ Missions brainstorming and promotion

____ Help with Missions Festival Day (end of October)

____ Help with "Missions Moms Information Packet" (Sept.–Oct.)

____ Be a missions representative for your small group (coordinate correspondence, pray, send packages from your group to your missionary)

Newsletter

____ Writing; list area(s) of interest:

____ Graphic arts

____ Editing/Proofreading

____ Typing/Word Processing

Platform

____ Help organize the up-front activities on speaker weeks (a subcommittee position which requires one monthly meeting and phone calls)

____ Set up and take down sound equipment at Moms and More on a regular basis (training provided)

____ Tape speakers

____ Write skits

Prayer

____ Be on a prayer team (circle one):   on a regular basis   for special events
____ Help with special prayer events (e.g., prayer breakfast, concert of prayer)

Program Performance

____ Skits
____ Video
____ Slide show
____ Vocal music (circle): alto soprano soloist group singer
____ Instrumental music (specify instrument):
____ Speaking spots (circle):   testimony   dramatic reading   poetry
____ Demonstrate/Tell (specify topic):
____ Other (please specify):
____ Emcee speaker weeks

Service Projects/Social Concerns

____ I have an interest in service projects
____ I have an interest in social concerns
____ I will help plan a craft day
____ I will teach a craft on craft day (specify)

Special Events

____ Help coordinate a special event (a subcommittee position which requires planning and implementing a brunch, special day, etc.)
____ Help plan a Birthday Party for Jesus
____ I will help in the following area for a special event:
____ Promotion
____ Ticket sales
____ Platform
____ Hospitality
____ Hostessing
____ Decorations
____ Food preparation

General Help

____ Graphic arts
____ Calligraphy
____ Sewing/fabrics
____ Nonprofessional still photography
____ Typing/word processing
____ Phone calling
____ Organization/administration
____ Finance
____ Bulletin board preparation
____ Other (please specify) _____

Thank you so much for taking the time to complete this survey. We rely heavily on this survey to find volunteers for the many areas of service necessary to help Moms & More function as a vital minstry. May God give you joy and blessings as you serve him here, or anywhere!

SCHOLARSHIP APPLICATION

The Committee solicits contributions to a scholarship fund and will give aid as money is available. Our policy is to provide up to one half the cost of a room for four, to women who have a definite financial need, on a first-come, first-served basis.

DEADLINE FOR APPLYING IS: _____

Name _____ Phone _____

Address_____ City _____ Zip _____

Marital Status_____ Number of dependent children _____

Place of employment_____

Have you received a scholarship before?_____

Please state reason(s) you feel you need aid: _____

_____

_____

_____

Name a friend who can verify: _____

Address _____ Phone _____

MAIL APPLICATION TO:

We may need to call you. When is the best time to reach you? _____
You will be notified of the decision by mail by _____. If *accepted*, you will receive an acceptance slip *that must accompany your registration.*

- -

I WOULD BE WILLING TO WORK AS:

      Hostess at large   _____   Small group leader_____

      Registration help   _____   Small group room hostess _____

      Other   _____

Name _____ Phone _____

(If *accepted* and you would like to help, this section *only* will be sent to coordinators.)

BREAKAWAY EVALUATION

Your comments about *Breakaway* are valuable to us! Please help us by completing the following evaluation and filling in the information that will assist us in preparing for next year.

Name _____ Phone _____

Address _____
                                                          City   State   Zip

Comment on *Breakaway's* strengths:

_____
_____
_____

What improvements for *Breakaway* would you suggest?

_____
_____
_____

Suggested seminar topics for next year:

_____
_____
_____

How did you hear about *Breakaway*?

_____ Church Bulletin   _____ Radio

_____ Christian Courier   _____ Friend

_____ Women's Ministry Mailing   _____ Poster

_____ Other _____

Marital Status:

____ Married   ____ Single   ____ Divorced   ____ Widowed

Age Group:

____ 18–25   ____ 26–35   ____ 36–45   ____ 46–55

____ 56–65   ____ 66–75   ____ 76–85   ____ 86–95

Children (please indicate how many on each line that applies)

_____ pre-schooler   _____ secondary

_____ elementary   _____ college/adult

Are you employed outside the home? _____ yes   _____ no

I am interested in helping with *Breakaway* 19____. (check one)

_____ yes   _____ no